On Her Shoulders

Collected Essays
on Women Playwrights from the Past

New Perspectives Theatre Company

Printed in the United States of America

First Printing, 2017

ISBN 978-0-692-84914-9

Library of Congress Control Number: 2017904208

ON HER SHOULDERS is produced by the New Perspectives Theatre Company,
in association with The School of Drama at the New School.
It is under the leadership of Melissa Attebery and Melody Brooks, with support from
associate producer Kristin Heckler.

Special thanks to Deborah Constantine for the book design and typesetting.

To order additional copies, please visit our website at www.nptnyc.org

Table of Contents

The Convent of Pleasure
by Margaret Cavendish

Directed by **Elyse Singer**
Dramaturgy by **Melissa Conkling**
Assistant Director: **Whitney Gail Aronson**

SPECIAL INTRODUCTION BY
Dr. Lisa Walters, President
International Margaret Cavendish Society
Friday, March 28, 2014

Mad Madge! by Melissa Conkling

Margaret Cavendish, Duchess of Newcastle-upon-Tyne was born to Thomas and Elizabeth Lucas near Colchester, England in 1623. The Lucases were an aristocratic family with tight Royalist ties. She did not receive a formal education, but did have access to scholarly libraries and was an avid reader. She became one of England's most prolific authors, publishing under her own name when most women did so anonymously. She was a playwright, poet, philosopher, essayist, as well as a writer of biographies, romantic prose, an autobiographical memoir, and one of the earliest examples of science fiction.

As the painfully shy youngest of eight children, Margaret spent extensive time with her older siblings, particularly her sisters, even as they started their own families. Her first efforts at writing were what she called her baby books. She wrote 16 of these books, the shortest of which was two or three quires of paper [50-75 pages]. The more she wrote the more she desired to excel in literature. She benefited greatly from regular conversations with her middle brother John, an established scholar and founding member of the Royal Society. Since her father passed away when she was very young, she grew up watching her mother manage the household finances and landholdings in addition to running the household and other tasks expected of an aristocratic wife. Her mother took pride in such activities and from childhood Margaret was instilled with a respect for strong women and an affinity for sisterhood which would affect her greatly as an adult.

As tensions mounted between Royalists and Parliamentarians, her close family became more strained. It was then that Margaret asked her mother to allow her to become a maid of honor for Queen Henrietta Maria. Margaret had come to idolize the Queen after her heroic actions upon her return to England just before the Civil War broke out. Despite the protests of her siblings (who did not think she was mature enough and feared that she would struggle in this new setting), her mother conceded, and Margaret went to live at the Queen's court in Oxford. For the first few years, though never truly happy or at home there, Margaret survived with regular visits from her nearby family members, despite having to give up her beloved writing. Soon however, as the war progressed, the Queen and her court were exiled to Paris. Deeply unhappy and homesick, Margaret never acclimated to court life and chose to withdraw from others, especially men, to avoid making any grievous social errors and to escape the confines of marriage, which she, along with many young women of her time, feared greatly.

At 22, Margaret was perhaps the unlikeliest lady at court to gain the affection of the most prominent English nobleman outside of the royal family when Marquess (later Duke) William Cavendish of Newcastle joined the court in exile. Nearly thirty years her senior, he quickly took a liking to the socially awkward outcast. Cavendish was an important patron of the arts in England and was also a poet and playwright. As their courtship began, he showered her with love poetry and soon encouraged her to rekindle her childhood passion for writing, just as he had encouraged his daughters from his first marriage despite the fact that writing was not prudent for young ladies of their class. The two also became the center of many rumors and controversies and the experience would give Margaret a lasting distaste for court life. After their marriage, on a return trip to England to petition for the return of William's properties, Margaret published her first book, *Poems and Fancies* in 1653. Aware of the reaction the public might have to a woman writer, the preface of the book addressed her female readership:

> *Condemn me not as a dishonour of your sex, for setting forth this work;*
> *for it is harmless and free from all dishonestly; I will not say from vanity,*
> for that is so natural to our sex as it were unnatural not to be so.

William and Margaret relocated to Antwerp, where she found herself playing hostess to her husband's renowned philosophical salons with famous thinkers of the day, including Thomas Hobbes, Rene Descartes,

Marin Mersenne, Pierre Gassendi, and Kenelm Digby. This association greatly expanded Margaret's writing interests in a range of genres, including philosophy, and she became a pioneer in science fiction with her book *The Description of a New World, Called the Blazing World* (1666).

Margaret was known as an eccentric, often dressing in peculiar clothes that set her apart from the rest of the crowd (which was in fact her aim). She earned the nickname "Mad Madge," and Samuel Pepys, the famous diarist, referred to her as "a mad, conceited, ridiculous woman." She died unexpectedly on December 15, 1673 at the age of fifty. Throughout her life, criticism of Margaret Cavendish outweighed praise and yet she continued to write. She published 22 works during her lifetime, and her modern reputation is of a truly remarkable woman. With many different facets to her personality, public life and private life, Margaret Cavendish, Duchess of Newcastle, as a woman and as a writer, remains something of an enigma to this day.

1. Kellett, Katherine R. "Performance, Performativity, and Identity in Margaret Cavendish's *The Convent of Pleasure*," *Studies in English Literature, 1500-1900* 48, no. 2 (2008): 419-442.

Out of the Closet at Last by Melissa Conkling
Edited by Melody Brooks

One of the most prolific writers in the early modern period, Margaret Cavendish developed a reputation for eccentricity that began in the 17th century and remains in force today. A wealthy Royalist, she spent most of her adult life writing, experimenting with—and stretching the bounds of—genres as diverse as autobiography, biography, oration, poetry, utopian fiction, science writing, and drama. Although much of Cavendish's work has inspired a renaissance of critical attention, only recently has her large body of difficult-to-classify plays (19 in all) awarded Cavendish much notice. The critical neglect of these plays has in part to do with the question of exactly how dramatic these writings, which have only recently begun to be produced, actually are. Yet despite Cavendish's decision not to produce her plays, they do not fit neatly into the genre of closet drama either, "a term," Anne Shaver argues, "for plays deliberately written to be read in one's 'closet' or private room; it is not a term appropriately applied to plays that simply were not produced." Instead, her plays comprise a spectacular (and usually subversive) hybridity of theatrical conventions, including pastoral romance, cross-dressing, and masque, stubbornly resisting classification."[1]

Upon her marriage to William Cavendish in 1645, at the age of 22, Margaret found herself playing hostess to his salon known as the "Cavendish Circle." It included some of the most famous thinkers of the day—Thomas Hobbes, Rene Descartes, Marin Mersenne, et al.—and exposed her to the latest philosophical and scientific theories. In the frontispiece of her 1656 publication, *Natures Pictures Drawn by Fancies Pencil to the Life*, she expresses what she feels about being allowed in the inner circle:

> Thus in this Semy-Circle, wher they sitt;
> Telling of Tales of pleasure & of witt
> Here you may read without sinn or Crime
> And how more innocently pass your tyme.

Although immersion in this intellectual world did broaden the range of her writing, these great men would not critically engage with Margaret directly. In her book *Philosophical Letters*, she instead debates their views in the form of a correspondence between herself and a fictional third person. How frustrating must it have been for this brilliant woman to have a seat at the table, but not a voice!

Although a few other English women had published books of poetry before Margaret, she is apparently the first to have written specifically (and prolifically across genres) *for* publication. She clearly expected attacks however, because extensive prefaces to her publications contain a preemptive defense, excusing her lack of education and acknowledging that it was "imprudent" for a woman to write.

It was her husband who inspired her to take up playwriting, instilling in her the confidence to attempt the dramatic arts through the reading of some of his own plays. The exact dates of her plays are unknown; two volumes were published in 1662 and 1668. But it is clear from surviving letters that she had begun writing plays no later than 1656. And she was, perhaps, most critical of her dramatic works, referring to them in the preface to her first volume of plays (*Plays Written* 1662), as "dull dead statues" and fearing they would be "hissed off from the Stage."

Beyond this fear, she gives no reason for making the choice to not have her plays performed. Maybe it was simply her insecurity, or because the theatres were just reopening in England, or that she admittedly took no pains to follow the strict neoclassical ideals that were *de rigueur* on the continent. It seems very likely, however, that she created these pieces to express thoughts and ideas that would never have been allowed on stage at the time, but would provoke debate in the intellectual salons that were common in her own home and among her peers. While the deliberation over her intentions and whether the plays are "suitable" for live performance continues today, it is clear these scripts are much more substantial than she was ever willing to assert publically. Most notably, Cavendish wrote three plays—T*he Female Academy* (1662), *Bell in Campo* (1662), and *The Convent of Pleasure* (1668)—in which she creates utopian heroines who take women's removal from the public (patriarchal) sphere to extremes, and construct new spaces in which women wield political power and authority.

The *Convent of Pleasure* begins much like any standard Restoration sex farce, but both style and content quickly make it clear it is anything but. In this play, women take charge of their own destinies. The characters voice a fear and loathing of the patriarchal structure, in which young women become the property of men who can do as they please with their "servant." The play rejects the status quo and instead creates a female-centric world in a location—the convent—whose utopian potential lies in its ability to house female power and autonomy unthinkable in other social settings. The convent's strict exclusionary rules and its cultural associations also establish a homoerotic context which remains fixed until the very end of the play.

The use of masque in much of the third and fourth acts—while seemingly outdated even at the time—is a powerful tool for exploring the political, social, and sexual/gender concepts of the play. The ladies' first performance mirrors their autonomous state. By their last pastoral they have been persuaded to return to a heterosexual norm. Gone are the "Varieties of pleasure" explored earlier in the play and the status quo is once again imposed. It is this ending (along with the mix of styles) that have confounded scholars and dramaturgs alike. And similar uncertainties in her other plays have added to the criticism, derision and diminution of her work as a dramatist down through the years.

We must let Cavendish herself have the last word as to her 17th Century intentions, in a statement in her epistle to her 1668 volume of plays: "I regard not so much the present as future Ages, for which I intend all my Books." With the current interest in and scholarship devoted to her work, she might finally get the attention and acclaim that she deserves.

Marriage is the tomb of Wit
—Margaret Cavendish

A Bold Stroke for a Wife
by Susanna Centlivre

Directed by **Rebecca Patterson**
Dramaturgy by **Tasha Gordon-Solomon**

Monday, December 16, 2013

A Bold Stroke of the Pen!
excepted from endnotes: Source: *Drama Criticism*, ©2005 Gale Cengage

SUSANNA CENTLIVRE was an English dramatic writer and actress, born about 1667. At sixteen she married the nephew of Sir Stephen Fox, and on his death she married an officer named Carroll, who was killed in a duel. Left in poverty, in 1700 she began to support herself by writing for the stage; some of her early plays are signed S. Carroll.

By number of performances, Centlivre could fairly be called the most successful English dramatist after William Shakespeare and before the twentieth century. Like her more famous counterpart, Aphra Behn, Centlivre suffered the prejudices, slights, and outright attacks peculiar to the station of the woman writer, but her plays lasted much longer and were performed much more frequently than those of Behn. Because her works are better performed than read, she was long dismissed by critics. Recent recognition of her theatrical skill and interest in her unique perspective as a female Whig dramatist have returned Centlivre to prominence as a major playwright of the early eighteenth century.

The facts of Centlivre's birth remain in dispute, but the standard version identifies her as the child of William and Anne Freeman of Lincolnshire, baptized in 1669. According to some, Mr. Freeman was a supporter of Cromwell prior to the Restoration, living in Ireland as an exile at the time of Susanna's birth. Biographer and friend Abel Boyer believed she was born to a Mr. Rawkins, of lower estate than Mr. Freeman. Documentary evidence exists to support both stories but confirm neither. Her early years are clouded by legend: Boyer refers to the "gay Adventures" of her youth "over which we shall draw a Veil," he adds. John Mottley, an acquaintance of Centlivre's tells in her biography that a young Susanna, fleeing a wicked stepmother, was picked up weeping at the side of a road by a Cambridge student, Anthony Hammond, who secreted her in his college rooms—allowing her to get a brief, second-hand university education. William Chetwood, another acquaintance, agreed that Centlivre fled her stepmother but wrote that she joined a troupe of traveling players.

Boyer helped her launch her career in 1700, with the production of the tragicomic play *The Perjur'd Husband* at the Drury Lane Theatre. For the next two decades Centlivre worked steadily at playwriting, though she published her first several plays anonymously. Even her first major success was released without her name attached; *The Gamester* (1705) did so well at Lincoln's Inn Fields that it was used two months later to open the new Haymarket Theatre. In 1706 Centlivre offered her play *Love at a Venture* to Colley Cibber, who was managing the Drury Lane Theatre, but Cibber rejected it. When he produced a very similar play, *The Double Gallants* (1707), under his own name, Centlivre had little recourse, but when Cibber's plagiarism was publicized he was roundly criticized. In the meantime, Centlivre had taken the play to the Duke of Grafton's servants, a troupe of strolling players then at Bath. Evidence suggests that she joined the troupe herself as a traveling performer.

Legend has it that the players performed *Alexander the Great* (some say *The Rival Queens*) for the court at Windsor, with Centlivre herself taking the title role. It was as Alexander, the story goes, that Centlivre first attracted the notice of one of the Queen's cooks, Joseph Centlivre. After their wedding on April 23, 1707, the couple lived at Buckingham Court, Spring Gardens, which was Centlivre's home for the rest of her life.

Although she was now financially secure, Centlivre continued to write plays, though not without difficulty. Her next play, *The Busie Body* (1709), was nearly rejected by Drury Lane and contemporary newspapers document the actors' contempt for "a silly thing wrote by a Woman." Centlivre's confidence in pressing the play was well-founded; it became one of her most successful works, winning the praise of Richard Steele in *The Tatler* and enjoying command performances at court in the subsequent decade. Her next few plays were beset by further tensions with actors, exacerbated by remarks attributed to her in *The Female Tatler*, complaining of their lack of respect and gratitude. Centlivre denied ever making such statements, but the damage was done. Centlivre's Whiggish politics, about which she became increasingly open, further created problems for theater companies eager to avoid censure from Queen Anne's Tory government. In 1714 she dedicated *The Wonder* to Prince George Augustus of the House of Hanover, Duke of Cambridge, in another show of Whig sympathies. Her faith was well-placed: the Duke soon became King George I, and the play became one of the most popular of the eighteenth century (and in which, as the jealous husband, David Garrick found one of his best parts.) She wrote two political satires in 1715, both of which were repressed by the Master of Revels, and a tragedy, *The Cruel Gift*, in 1716.

Her Whig sympathies, anti-Catholic beliefs, and commercial success also made Centlivre a target for the era's keenest satirist, Alexander Pope. He lampooned her in the character of the playwright Phoebe Clinket in the farce *Three Hours after Marriage* (1717), which he wrote with John Gay and John Arbuthnot; five years after her death he included her in his catalogue of dullards, *The Dunciad* (1728). Centlivre produced her final major comedy in 1718; *A Bold Stroke for a Wife* successfully played at Lincoln's Inn Fields that year, and continued to be a favorite actor's vehicle well into the next century. Her health began to decline in the next year, and she wrote only one more play, the stridently political comedy *The Artifice* (1722), which was not a popular success.

Critical opinion of Centlivre as a minor dramatist restricted the study of her works to *The Busie Body, The Wonder*, and *A Bold Stroke for a Wife* well into the twentieth century, but modern reassessments of her talent and importance have begun to increase the standard Centlivre canon. The first significant critical study of Centlivre is John Wilson Bowyer's biography of 1952 (*The Celebrated Mrs. Centlivre*), which continues to be a primary reference on the author's life and works. Centlivre's treatment of women is a primary theme of scholarship, especially her depiction of marriage and how women fare in finding and surviving a husband. The intersection of gender and political themes has brought renewed attention to *The Gamester* and *The Basset Table*, which contain some of Centlivre's most progressive female characters. As Victoria Warren suggests, the unsettling combination of women and money in those plays spoke directly to Centlivre's predicament as a woman compelled for much of her life to write for her livelihood. Centlivre died on December 1, 1723, and is buried at St. Paul's in Covent Garden.

Broad Shoulders!
by Tasha Gordon-Solomon

A Bold Stroke for a Wife is written in the tradition of the restoration comedy of the seventeenth and early eighteenth centuries. Following a period of cultural Puritanism, these plays reveled in sharp satire of social mores, and racy, bawdy comedy. *A Bold Stroke* reflects the later restoration comedies, which were geared toward an increasingly middle-class and female audience. During this time, the tamer sentimental comedy, was emerging as a genre. The play can also be seen as a satiric response to these plays and their preoccupation with morality and virtue.

The restoration period was a milestone for women in theater. It saw the emergence of professional female playwrights, beginning with Aphra Behn, whose first production corresponded with Centlivre's birth. During this time, woman actors replaced the convention of men playing different genders on stage. Yet despite this progressive environment, *A Bold Stroke* raises some feminist questions for a contemporary audience. Most of the scenes are occupied by men and the story has a male protagonist. We follow Colonel Feignwell as he tries to get consent to marry Anne. Meanwhile, she spends most of the time relatively inactive, waiting for him to win her freedom from her guardians and access to her inheritance. And this freedom can only be obtained by transferring her charge to yet another male figure, a husband. This irony is encapsulated when Anne says, "He promised to set me free; and on that condition, I promised to make him master of that freedom."

However, a closer look at the play reveals the more subtle ways Centlivre commented on social structures themselves. Centlivre's work had to navigate an environment that was less than ideal. A number of her plays were not published under her (female) name, because publishers feared they wouldn't be successful. The rise in celebrity actors mostly affected men. Centlivre managed to create a play that was a commercial success, while simultaneously subverting the patriarchal structure she was working within.

One target of *A Bold Stroke* is the marriage contract, which is rendered increasingly ridiculous throughout the play. The legalities around marriage at the time were so inconsistent, Britain passed the Marriage Duty acts of the late 1690s in an attempt to lend more formality to the institution. Centlivre herself is believed to have been married three times. In the play, the negotiations among the groom and guardians are based on such bizarre premises, they undermine the validity of the contract itself. Feignwell only gains consent under false pretences, often obtaining written permission that does not even use his real name. This gives the contract, and by extension the institution questionable legitimacy.

Centlivre goes even further to envision a more egalitarian version of marriage. Literary critic Vivian Davis proposes that the play "offers an important alternative model for marital relations, one in which male and female parties are not contract negotiators subject to legally inscribed gender hierarchies, but enthusiastic costars on a shared stage of possibility." She sites as an example, the final scene, in which Miss Lovely pretends to be experiencing a divine revelation in order to obtain the consent of her final guardian. Davis notes it is Miss Lovely who takes the lead here, hilariously acting out an ecstatic religious possession, while Feignwell takes on the supporting role of straight man.

In fact, the humor in the aforementioned exchange is also derived from Anne's innuendo-filled language. ("...and now I see myself within thy arms, yea, I am becoming bone of thy bone and flesh of thy flesh.") From her first lines in the play, Anne struggles to have ownership over her body. This is manifested in her argument with the religious Prims who make her replace her fashionable, revealing dress with a conservative Quaker outfit. These struggles to express her sexuality in both her words and wardrobe (not to mention in her choice of partner), read today as a clear cry for physical agency.

Finally, although men occupy most of the space in the play, it doesn't make the female characters less important. The four guardians are portrayed as incompetent, and deluded, while Anne is more intelligent and rational. Her awareness that her best option is to find a husband she likes, who will give her as much freedom as she can get, is quite level-headed and realistic, given the circumstance. All the men in the play engage in lying, cheating and posturing. Even if Feignwell is driven by more pure intentions, he still spends most of the play double-dealing. Aside from her moment of pretend in the last scene, Anne tells the truth throughout the play. She sharply calls out the Prims on their hypocrisy and she tells her guardians exactly what she thinks of them, to their faces. No one else in the play is so consistently straightforward. Although she may not have the most lines, Centlivre is telling us to pay the most attention to what Anne says.

And we must pay attention to what Centlivre says—whether it is her call for individual liberty, her incisive social commentary, or the delightfully entertaining story she tells—which deserves to be heard many times over.

Want is the mistress of invention.
—Susanna Centlivre

—

House of Desires
by Sor Juana Inés de la Cruz
translation by Catherine Boyle

Directed by **Melody Brooks**
Dramaturgy by **Heather Violanti**

Friday, December 4, 2015

The Tenth Muse by Heather Violanti

Sor Juana Inés de la Cruz (c.1651-1695) defied 17th century conventions to become one of the most prominent playwrights, poets, and scholars in the colony of New Spain (now Mexico)—until those conventions destroyed her.

She was born Juana Ramírez de Asbaje in 1651, in San Miguel de Nepantla, a town near Mexico City. Her mother, Isabel Ramírez de Santillana, was a *criolla*, meaning she was of Spanish descent but had been born in the colony. Her father, Pedro Manuel de Asbaje y Vargas Manchuca, was a Spanish soldier from the Basque region. On the surface, it might seem an advantageous match. In the evolving social and racial hierarchy of New Spain, *criollas* sought marriage with Europeans to raise their standing. Isabel and Pedro, however, were not married, and Pedro abandoned the family after Juana was born.

Both Juana's social background and gender could have kept her at the fringes of society, but she hungered for education. At age three, she followed her sister to school and demanded to be taught to read. At age six or seven, when she first heard about the universities of Mexico City, she begged her mother to allow her to study there. When she was told only males could attend, she wanted her mother to disguise her as a boy. As this was impossible she taught herself from her maternal grandfather's library.

In 1664, at age 13, Juana's precocious scholarship and beauty had caught the attention of the new viceroyal couple. She was brought to their glittering court in Mexico City and became Vicereine Doña Leonor Carreto's favorite lady-in-waiting. Juana's poems, wit, and good looks charmed courtiers, but she soon tired of the artifice of court life. She wanted to devote herself to writing and learning. The only way this was possible for a woman was to enter a convent. In 1667, dreaming of a scholarly life, Juana joined the Barefoot Carmelites of St. Joseph, but their rigorous asceticism proved too much for her delicate health. She returned to court briefly to recover. Then, in 1669, she entered the Convent of Saint Paula of the Order of St. Jerome, where she would remain for the rest of her life. This order initially allowed Juana the freedom to pursue her scholastic and literary ambitions. She could write, study, host salons, and hold court with visiting dignitaries and governing officials.

Juana began her literary career as a poet. By 1676, her song poems were being performed at church services and garnering acclaim. She was particularly known for her *villancicos*, a type of sung poem, or carol, with its roots in peasant songs. Spanish Golden Age poets such as Lope de Vega had made *villancicos* the height of fashion. Juana expanded the stylish *villancico* form, blending the expected lyricism and wordplay with surprising new elements—the language and cultural life of New Spain, everything from African dialect to indigenous legends and dances. She also began to develop her dramatic skills, creating songs that resembled miniature plays, complete with complex plots and rich characters. In 1677, her first collection of songs was published—the *Villancicos de San Pedro Nolasco*.

By the 1680's, Juana was at the height of her influence and literary powers, daring to publicly question male authority. In 1681, she wrote an impassioned "Spiritual Self Defense" criticizing Father Antonio Núñez de Miranda, her former confessor at the convent. Miranda had questioned the right of women to study and write poetry. In the "Self Defense," Juana argued for women to be educated on equal footing with men:

> "Do women not have rational souls like men? Then, why should they not also enjoy the privilege of the enlightenment of letters? Is a woman's soul not as open to God's grace and glory as a man's? Then, why should it not be open to learning and the sciences, which are lesser than the glories of God? What divine revelation, what ruling of reason created such a severe law for us?"

Juana also began to write plays during this productive time. Her first comedy, *Los empeños de una casa* (was written in 1683 to celebrate the arrival of a new viceroyal couple in New Spain. In *House of Desires*, Juana had toyed with the conventions of Golden Age comedies, re-examining the Spanish code of honor from a female perspective. This play's success led to her next dramatic work, *Amor es más labyrinto* (*Love is a Greater Labyrinth*), a re-telling of the Minotaur myth written in collaboration with Juan de Guevara in 1689. She may have written, or at least contributed to, a third play, *La segunda Celestina* (*The Second Celestina*), a play written shortly before *House of Desires* and referenced during its intermission entertainments.

By the last decade of the 17th century, Juana began to tread on dangerous ground. The political and social climate in New Spain, while always precarious for women, became even more uncertain due to economic and governmental instability. In 1690, Bishop Manuel Fernández de Santa Cruz published Juana's critique of a controversial sermon on the forms of Christ's love—without her permission. The Bishop prefaced it with a damning letter by "Sor Filotea" (actually the Bishop himself writing under a female pen name), urging Juana to abandon intellectual discourse and pursue less ambitious, less worldly activities more appropriate for a nun. In 1691, Juana responded with her famous "Respuesta de la poetica a la muy ilustre Sor Filotea de la Cruz," ("The Poet's Answer to the Most Illustrious Sister Filotea de la Cruz)—an astute and heartfelt defense of women's right to education and her own right to live life as she chose.

After the *Respuesta*, however, Juana lost her freedoms. Under pressure from convent and Church authorities, she gave up her library, renounced writing, and wrote a renewal of her religious vows in her own blood. At the same time, she wrote out her death certificate in blood—asking her sisters to fill in the date when the time came. They had not long to wait. Physically weakened and spiritually broken, Sor Juana fell ill while nursing her fellow sisters during an outbreak of plague. She died on April 17, 1695.

The high regard in which Sor Juana was held is reflected in the eulogies to her by more than 60 poets of Spain and New Spain. These tributes were collected by Juan Ignacio de Castorena y Ursúa and published five years after her death in *Fama y obras posthumas del Fénix de México dezima musa, poetisa americana, Sor Juana Inés de la Cruz* (A celebration of and posthumous works by the Phoenix of Mexico and Tenth Muse, the Mexican poet, Sor Juana Inés de la Cruz).

Seeing And Not Seeing: *House Of Desires* In Context **by Heather Violanti**

Sor Juana Inés de la Cruz (c.1651-1695) is considered one of the last great authors of the *Siglo de oro*, the "Golden Age" of literature that flourished in the Spanish-speaking world from the mid-sixteenth century to the last decades of the seventeenth. *House of Desires* ranks among Sor Juana's masterpieces, reflecting both her feminist perspective and her desire to create great literature in the idiom of the "new" world, Mexico.

House of Desires, first performed on October 4, 1683 in Mexico City, was part of a *festejo*, a festival featuring a play, songs, and interactive performances. The *House of Desires festejo* is believed to be the only one to have survived in its entirety. It honors the then-current viceroy (governor) of New Spain, Don Tomás Antonio de la Cerda, and celebrates the arrival of a new archbishop, Francisco de Aguiar y Seijias, into Mexico City. Ironically, the bishop preached against the evils of theatre.

Following the traditions of the form, the *festejo* begins with a *loa*, brief dramatic/poetic piece typically written in praise of a saint or official. Sor Juana, who had excelled at crafting *loas* since childhood, wrote a song poem in which Merit, Diligence, Fortune, and Chance compete to see who is the greatest of joys.

Another element of the *festejo* was the *sainete*, a short interlude performed between acts of the main play, whose themes echoed those of the play. Sor Juana used the *sainetes* for *House of Desires* to comment on life in New Spain. The first *sainete*, the *Sainete del palacio* (*Sainete of the Palace*), was a veiled critique on the artificiality of court life—prior to becoming a nun, Sor Juana had spent formative years in the viceregal court of Mexico City. In the *Sainete of the Palace*, the allegorical figures of Love, Respect, Courtesy, and Kindness compete to win the disdain of the palace ladies—only to be told, in the end, that they do not deserve such a dubious honor.

The play's other *sainete*, simply called *Sainete segundo* (*Second Sainete*), ranks among the most innovative moments in Spanish theatre. Reflecting the Golden Age obsession with metatheatricality—the audience's awareness that they are watching a play—this sainete features two "audience members," Arias and Muñiz, who criticize the play they are watching. In a sly wink to the prejudices of New Spanish audiences, who were trained to think anything written in Spain was superior, they complain that it is not funny enough and is not as good as Spanish plays. They dismiss the play as *mestizo* (of mixed race). In an ever slyer wink to the prejudices against women playwrights, they attribute it to a male contemporary of Sor Juana, Acevedo (since a female author would be unthinkable, however much they dislike the play). Then, "Acevedo" himself appears, is hissed at by the audience, and dies of shame because his play has failed.

The performance concluded with a *sarao*, a masquerade with music and dance. Sor Juana concluded *House of Desires* with the *Sarao de cuatro naciones (Sarao of Four Nations)*, an exploration of the complex relationships between the "old" and "new" world, between colonizer and colony. In this piece, four "nations"—Spain, Africa, Italy, and New Spain—comment on the play itself as well as their own cultures.

House of Desires plays with the conventions of Spanish Golden Age comedy, which, like the comedies of Shakespeare, revolved around complicated love triangles, mistaken identities, and intrigue. Sor Juana both celebrates and parodies these conventions to craft a poetical exploration of the meaning of desire—and the place of women in society. The play's very title—*Los empeños de una casa* in Spanish—alludes to the title of a popular comedy by Pedro Calderón de la Barca, *Los empeños de un acaso (The Trials of Chance)*. By playing with words, Sor Juana immediately acknowledges—and subverts—the work of the male "masters" who have preceded her.

Calderón was known for his "cloak and dagger" comedies, which featured elaborate love plots, elopements, disguises, witty word play, and thrilling sword fights. Sor Juana uses all these elements in *House of Desires* and makes them her own. Notably, it is women—Doña Ana and Leonor—who drive much of the intrigue. The play's great comic moment—during which Carlos' crafty servant, Castaño, disguises himself in Leonor's clothes—honors the cloak and dagger tradition while adding a distinctly feminist perspective, making the audience aware of what it is like to experience the critical male gaze.

With its emphasis on mistaken identity, and its play on seeing and not seeing, *House of Desires* urges Sor Juana's audience to notice what they might otherwise overlook—the real emotions obscured by the strict Spanish "honor code" (which emphasized the *appearance* of virtue above all else), and the talented women like Sor Juana, made invisible by a time and place that offered few opportunities for them to succeed. Indeed, many scholars have pointed out that the central character of Leonor, a beautiful woman with a brilliant mind, bears many similarities to Sor Juana herself.

Translator Catherine Boyle concludes: "Writing from her convent, invisible at the performance of the play, Sor Juana writes herself into it; she forces us to see her."

Aristotle could have known so much more if he cooked.
—Sor Juana Inés de la Cruz

A Taste of Honey
by Shelagh Delaney

Directed by **Ludovica Villar-Hauser**
Dramaturgy by **Elizabeth Whitney**
Assistant to the Director: **Teresa Lotz**

Monday, September 16, 2013

Shelagh Delaney: A Lighthouse for Women Playwrights
by Elizabeth Whitney

Shelagh Delaney (1938 2011) was born in Salford, Lancashire, England, a working-class, industrial setting that inspired her to write her first and most notable play, *A Taste of Honey*. Delaney's father was a bus inspector and her mother was—like many women in their world—a mother. While Delaney lived much of her later life in London, she remained emotionally attached to her roots in Salford. In his 1966 essay, "A Taste of Honey and the Popular Play," Arthur K. Oberg notes that "One of the first things an audience notices about *A Taste of Honey* is the quickness and naturalness of the pace." Ostensibly, Oberg is referring to the colloquial, linguistic style of the piece, so famously derived from Shelagh Delaney's life experience growing up in Salford. However, this is a particularly intriguing comment in light of the fact that Delaney was only eighteen years old when she wrote *A Taste of Honey*, and we might surmise that she, like the environs which inspired her, was "a natural."

While her youthful promise received support from many—especially Joan Littlewood, who is credited with being a strong mentor in her early career during production of *A Taste of Honey*—she was also disdained or held in suspicion by many, including some from her hometown of Salford, who felt that her representation of them was less than favorable. It could be that her self-possessed and direct personality was surprising—in early television interviews, she does seem mature beyond her years.

Jeanette Winterson writes that Delaney was, "like a lighthouse, pointing the way and warning about the rocks underneath." Winterson's essay, titled, "My hero, Shelagh Delaney," argues that Delaney's early success unfairly eclipsed her later accomplishments. Given that her prolific career also included a series of television, film, and radio productions, a collection of short stories, and numerous awards, it hardly seems fair to write her off as a "one hit wonder." As Winterson suggests, Delaney did pave the way for other working-class and female playwrights, contributing a strong and much needed voice during the British Kitchen Sink Drama and New Wave eras.

Her screenplays include *The White Bus* (1967), directed by Lindsay Anderson, which she adapted from one of her short stories; *Charlie Bubbles* (1967) with Albert Finney (who also directed) and Liza Minnelli, about a successful young writer who returns home from London to Manchester and struggles to cope with his good fortune in the world of commonplace deprivation he encounters there; and *Dance With a Stranger*, Mike Newell's 1985 film, starring Miranda Richardson and Rupert Everett, about Ruth Ellis, who murdered her lover and in 1955 was the last woman to be executed in Britain. She also wrote a collection of stories and short nonfiction pieces, *Sweetly Sings the Donkey*, which was published when she was 24. Many of the pieces in the book were dramatized for a BBC radio series.

Delaney's positive representations of gays and working-class culture have influenced many artists, most notably The Smiths. Lead singer Morissey has stated, "I've never made any secret of the fact that at least 50 per cent of my reason for writing can be blamed on Shelagh Delaney." Her photo was featured on the cover of their 1987 album, *Louder than Bombs*, and direct quotes from her plays are found in many of their songs.

Curiously, little has been written about her life, and her public appearances and interviews were scarce in her later years, possibly of her own volition. We know that she was survived by a daughter and three grandchildren. She never married. She died from breast cancer at 72, in 2011.

A Taste of Honey: Kitchen Sink Patter That Dared
by Elizabeth Whitney

Shelagh Delaney was inspired to write *A Taste of Honey* at age 18 after a trip to Manchester to see Terrence Rattigan's *Variation on a Theme*. Delaney was bored and somewhat put-off by Rattigan's covert representation of homosexuality in the piece, and determined that she could do better. And she did—writing *A Taste of Honey* in just two weeks. It was first produced at the Theatre Royal Stratford East (1958), in an iconic production directed by Joan Littlewood that featured live jazz musicians, and later went on to Wyndam's Theatre in the West End (1959), and the Lyceum and Booth Theatres on Broadway in (1960).

A young, working-class woman with no formal training as a playwright, she turned to her rich surroundings in her home of Salford, Lancashire, England and the inherent musicality of the language she knew best to create a seminal piece of theatre. Delaney's work is located at the intersection of Kitchen Sink Drama and Music Hall Style. Kitchen Sink Dramas were part of a new wave of British theatre that addressed issues of social class using mundane settings and domestic issues, and Delaney's contemporaries included "angry young men" John Osborne, known best for *Look Back in Anger* (1956), and Arnold Wesker, who wrote *The Kitchen* (1950). Like *A Taste of Honey*, both of the aforementioned pieces were also made into films and entered into British popular culture as representative resistance to prior tokenizing, upper class depictions of working class culture.

Music Hall Style drew from a kind of vaudevillian low brow comedy and was marked by quick patter, evoking the spirit of a cabaret with multiple acts including jugglers, comedians, singers, and acrobats—for example, Delaney's staging includes characters dancing between scenes. We need look no further than the relationship between Helen and Jo to understand Music Hall Style. Helen is a woman who relies on her "fancy men" for financial subsistence, and eschews traditional motherhood, much as her daughter, Jo does later on in the play. Jo's disdain for her mother is palpable, surfacing in their tense interactions, but also manifesting in more complex ways, such as when she refers to pregnancy as cannibalistic, and later says, "I don't want to be a mother. I don't want to be a woman." Jo struggles against the limited conditions of her life—wanting something different yet without the means to attain it. Delaney skillfully uses the tensions between Jo and Helen to create an almost comedic relationship, as they alternate playing the "straight man." The stage directions indicate that the play opens with jazz music. As the characters enter, the patter begins immediately, and the mother and daughter team operate as a comedy duo, throwing dialogue at each other in quick response:

> HELEN: Well! This is the place.
> JO: And I don't like it.
> HELEN: When I find some place for us to live I have to consider something far more important than your feelings...the rent. It's all I can afford.
> JO: You can afford something better than this old ruin.

The parallel structure of the language is what makes them seem to operate like a well oiled machine. However, immediately following this exchange, a dynamic of alienation enters:

> HELEN: When you start earning you can start moaning.
> JO: Can't be soon enough for me...I'm cold and my shoes let water...What a place...And we're supposed to be living off of her immoral earnings.

Jo's reference to Helen in the third person is an important aside to her audience that establishes her independence, as at the end of the play when Helen breaks the fourth wall and directly addresses the audience, asking, "What would you do?" This self-awareness was a radical position for female characters, and part of what shocked so many theatre audiences. To see women onstage with agency that was not only self-reflective, but comically biting, was quite unlike other contemporary playwrights from the "angry young man" genre whose work, while in some ways addressing domestic issues, was always from a masculinist perspective.

Helen and Jo's relationship is only one aspect of the unique and progressive work that *A Taste of Honey* was for its time. Jo's romantic involvement with a black sailor on leave, while intended to progressively address interracial relationships, is not without its complications. His character, for example, has no name until near the end of the play. He is simply, "The Boy," which both erases him as an individual and emasculates his status as an adult man. He is also exoticized as 'a prince from darkest Africa,' which may be Jo's idea of humor, though still speaks to limited understandings of the African diaspora in Great Britain. Finally, "The Boy" seems to have internalized himself as part of the white imagination, saying to Jo, "Let me be Othello and you my Desdemona," which is hardly a generous reading of his character. It's a tough argument to make that this is a move toward political commentary, and remains to be understood as Delaney's well-intentioned but problematic attempt to progressively represent race onstage.

Geof, on the other hand, is more of a success for Delaney in terms of resisting cultural clichés—and likely this was more easily accomplished as whiteness was already part of her world view. An openly gay man—although that appears to be due more to others' assumptions than his admissions—he and Jo settle into their own domestic play, keeping house together and preparing for the birth of her child. Geof's very presence as a likeable character who attempts to care for Jo and expresses parental desire speaks against stereotypes, despite being referred to as 'nursemaid' and 'organ grinder's monkey' by Helen, and 'Mary' and 'cuddles' by Peter.

Peter, Helen's alcoholic husband, is no more than an annoying necessity. He is required for financial assistance, and to a certain extent, catered to, although mostly he is an absence in this script, only noticed when he intrudes into the domestic space. Perhaps most importantly, Peter—in a way that is unique to his subject position as a heterosexual, white, middle-class male—functions in this piece as "other."

A Taste of Honey was a groundbreaking upstart that continues to surprise theatrical audiences. Delaney puts social class, racial identity, and sexuality in conversation with one another on stage with daring and forthright intention, and for that, we owe her a debt of gratitude.

> *Anything's hard to find if you go around looking for it with your eyes shut.*
> —Shelagh Delaney, from *The Lion in Love*

The Years Between
by Daphne du Maurier

Directed by **Mary McGinley**
Dramaturgy by **Susan Jonas**

Monday, November 18, 2013

Nothing Like a Dame! by Melody Brooks

Born in London on May 13, 1907, Daphne du Maurier came from a creative and highly successful family. She was the grand-daughter of the cartoonist and writer George du Maurier and daughter of Gerald, the most famous Actor Manager of his day. Gerald's sister was Sylvia Llewelyn Davies, whose five boys inspired JM Barrie's *Peter Pan*; among those who came to watch Daphne and her two sisters' nursery performances of his "terrible masterpiece" was "Uncle Jim" Barrie himself. Each girl got the minimum of formal schooling necessary to prepare them for the "good marriage" none of them in fact wanted.

"Even among Edwardians, Gerald's sexual hypocrisy was notable. He longed for a son, never got one and made each daughter in turn his victim. And yet, after he died, Daphne—who refused to attend his funeral-quite literally wore his trousers for more than a decade. That seems emblematic. All his daughters were tomboys who invented heroic male alter egos... and only Daphne enjoyed successful long-term relationships with men..."[1]

Du Maurier began writing short stories in 1928; some were published in her great uncle William Comyns Beaumont's *Bystander* magazine. In 1931 her first novel, *The Loving Spirit* was published. It received rave reviews and further books followed. She married Major (later Lieutenant-General) Sir Frederick "Boy" Browning in 1932 and had two daughters and a son. Apparently, he demanded an introduction to Daphne on the strength of having read one of her novels. "Here was a hero of the first world war, an ideal fantasy-figure. Daphne herself, after 10 weeks, proposed marriage... he was deeply conventional and unimaginative; she self-willed and essentially a loner. They were strangely matched."[2]

Rebecca, inspired by Daphne's discovery that her husband had had a previous lover who committed suicide, is generally regarded as her masterpiece. In the U.S. she won the National Book Award for favorite novel of 1938, voted by members of the American Booksellers Association. It was adapted for stage by du Maurier herself, as well as for the screen on multiple occasions. Several of her other novels also became films, including *Jamaica Inn, Frenchman's Creek, Hungry Hill,* and *My Cousin Rachel.* The Hitchcock film, *The Birds* (1963), is based on a treatment of one of her short stories, as is the film *Don't Look Now* (1973).

Though literary critics have rebuked du Maurier's writings for their lack of intellectual heft, admirers consider her a first-rate storyteller and mistress of suspense. She was often labeled a "romantic novelist" (a term she despised), though most of her books do not fit neatly into the stereotypical format of a romance novel. They rarely have a happy ending, and her brand of romanticism is often at odds with the sinister overtones and shadows of the paranormal she favored. In this, she has more in common with the "sensation novels" of Wilkie Collins, whom she admired. Sensation novels were precursors to modern detective fiction or suspense novels. Her biographer Margaret Forster wrote: "She satisfied all the questionable criteria of popular fiction, and yet satisfied too the exacting requirements of 'real literature.'" Her stories read like classic tales of terror and suspense but were written with a sure touch for character, imagery and suggestive meaning.

Thirteen forgotten short stories written in the 1920s were published in a new collection in May 2011. They reveal, perhaps better than anything, that du Maurier was way ahead of her time and far from an insipid romance novelist. One of them, *The Doll*, is described as "gothic, suspenseful and macabre." It tells the story of a frustrated romance in which a young man discovers the girl he loves-also called Rebecca—will never accept his advances because she owns a life-size mechanical male doll. Her son, Kit Browning, who still lives in his mother's house, claims he would have liked to have teased her about it. "It's a very dark and disturbing story for someone who was 21 when she wrote it, and from the sort of background that she came from."

Du Maurier wrote only three plays. Her first was a successful adaptation of *Rebecca,* which opened at the Queen's Theatre in London on 5 March 1940, ultimately running for 357 performances after a transfer to the

Strand. Her second play, *The Years Between* opened in January 1945, five months before VE Day, and ran for 617 performances. A film version was made in 1946 starring Michael Redgrave. Better known is her third play, *September Tide*, about a middle-aged woman whose artist son-in-law falls in love with her. It opened at the Aldwych on December 15, 1948 with Gertrude Lawrence in the lead, running for 267 performances and closing in early August 1949. It led to a close but ambiguous relationship with Lawrence.

In correspondence released to Forster by her family after Daphne's death, du Maurier explained to a trusted few her own unique slant on her sexuality: her personality, she explained, comprised two distinct people—the loving wife and mother (the side she showed to the world) and the lover (a decidedly male energy) hidden to virtually everyone and the power behind her artistic creativity. According to the biography, du Maurier believed the male energy fueled her creative life as a writer.

Du Maurier was made a Dame Commander of the Order of the British Empire in 1969. She accepted but never used the title. Lady Browning; Dame Daphne du Maurier DBE, died at the age of 81 on April 19, 1989, at her home in Cornwall, in a region which had been the setting for many of her books. In accordance with her wishes, her body was cremated and her ashes were scattered on the cliffs near her home.

---

1. (Peter J. Conradi, reviewing *Daphne du Maurier and her Sisters: The Hidden Lives of Piffy, Bird and Bing*, by Jane Dunn, *Financial Times*, 3/1/13).
2. Ibid.

Daphne and Diana: Resisting Roles **by Susan Jonas D.F.A.**

Daphne du Maurier's private life has been the object of great speculation and sensationalism, much focused on to what degree, if at all, she acted on her lesbian inclinations, if indeed she had them. Armchair psychology has been applied to her penchant for trousers, her grudging relinquishment of youthful tomboyhood, and her periodic ambivalence about motherhood—all indicative of resistance to the limitations imposed by gender, not solely sexual preference. The most sensational allegation—that she had an affair with her father's ex-mistress, Gertrude Lawrence, was roundly challenged, both by the failure of the rumored evidential letters to appear, and by Lawrence's own daughter who insisted that while she would have no objection to her mother's alleged bisexuality, in fact the actress was voraciously "heterosexual to the point of nymphomania."[1] Many have asserted that du Maurier went to great lengths to hide her lesbianism, but given that both of du Maurier's sisters were "out" lesbians living openly with their partners, there would have been little shock value. And the product of a theatrical family given to off-stage theatrics, she was scarcely averse to being provocative; at dinner parties she would ask siblings if they had considered incest.

Whatever her sexual inclinations and activities were, we may never know, but we do know she was deeply ambivalent about her role as a wife, mother and writer. She was drawn to solitude and in her letters often remarked that she dreaded the return home to Cornwall of her husband, who was often away at war and later lived in London. Yet despite their largely separate lives, they remained married for 33 years until his death in 1965. She confessed that she found motherhood a strain and left much of the care to her nanny, preferring to eat alone and to spend her evenings working. Yet in a letter to her friend, she faulted herself, saying, "It's people like me who have careers who really have bitched up the old relationship between men and women. Women ought to be soft and gentle and dependent. Disembodied spirits like myself are all wrong."[2] Of course, despite her self-censuring, she never considered giving up her work.

To her creation, Diana Wentworth,[3] she was much more forgiving, offering us a character who is far more attractive than unattractive. When she learns her husband's plane has crashed into the ocean, she is grief stricken but also admits: "I suddenly realized my life doesn't belong to him anymore; it's mine; I can do what I like with it. And, oh, Richard, that sudden sense of freedom—almost as if the years had rolled away and I was young again..."[4] Despite her insistence that she lacks all personal ambition, Diana becomes an effective and charismatic politician. And if Diana leaves the care of her home and child to the capable nanny and avuncular neighbor, she does not alienate her audience in so doing. She even finds love—with a man who offers her the kind of support she offered her husband.

Diana is torn between *oikos* and *polis*—domestic and public life, love and duty, nostalgia and a vision of the future, self-interest and responsibility—towards her husband, child, community, country. If du Maurier was struggling to reconcile her own desires and obligations, she was also investigating the role of women in her life and work at a moment when gender was of necessity being rapidly redefined, or perhaps more to the point, repackaged for convenience and economic use at a pivotal moment.

Consider the context. The role of women was defined by "science," religion and women's magazines as romanticized subservience to men and a biological imperative to motherhood. Then suddenly, with the advent of war, women were needed to quickly replenish the workforce as the men went "Over There." A massive government public relations effort aimed to convince women that they were both capable of and obligated to work, that it was essential to their men and their nation, but also to their very self-perception as women. Suddenly women flooded into all the workplaces from which they had been prohibited. They were being told they were contributing importantly, that they were patriots, even home-front heroes. No longer were their priorities dirty diapers, meal preparation, house-cleaning and making themselves attractive, in part by projecting helplessness. Then, with the end of the war, they were told to stand aside and allow the returning menfolk their rightful place as breadwinners. Women should again assume the pretty domestic poses that their menfolk saw as emblems of the nation they sought to preserve, not to mention validation of their manhood. (This expectation and sense of betrayal was no less powerful in this country after the Vietnam War.) But how could it have been expected that once women have tasted independence, productivity, and camaraderie, that they would cheerfully put on their aprons and make pies in their ticket-tacky houses?

Unquestionably *The Years Between* is of its time, and deliciously so for those of us who have a particular taste for the trembling lower lip and stiff upper lip of British theatre and film of the *Brief Encounter* ilk—a predilection I share with the director, Mary McGinley, who explains:

> The British imports, like *I Know Where I'm Going* and *Brief Encounter* held a special place. These romances did not just tell a love story. They told stories of love against the odds. Though many might be classed as war-time propaganda, they were imbued with a sense of strength necessary to carry on and rise above the situation. They were imbued with a sense of honor, duty and nobility. This had a great impact on me as a young girl and I saw love as something deeper than mere romance.

It is the bulwark theme of Western drama, from Orestes to Hamlet to Biff, "How to be a good man?" What is perhaps most alluring about this play is that it is the moral choice of a woman protagonist that is of utmost consequence, and though those choices have changed over time, the decisions are no less wrenching between work and home, love and honor, happiness and responsibility.

The Years Between is startlingly prescient about the conflicts that would, for coming decades, dominate discussion around gender roles, and though the seeds sown in post-war England bloomed into revolution twenty to thirty years later, can anyone think we are today close to resolving these enduring conflicts? And the painful estrangement of couples separated through war, who must renegotiate their roles—gender-related or not—is no less acute in 2013, nor is the profound sense of betrayal felt by those returning from fighting for a country that has moved on.

We may never know what Daphne du Maurier did in bed. It is much more significant to recognize what she did on paper; she used her own inner conflicts to explore and confront major social conflicts on a wide historical stage.

---

1. "Daphne's Terrible Secret," Michael Thornton *Mail Online* May 2007.
2. "Daphne's Dilemma," Lynn Barber, *The Independent*, March 14 1993.
3. It seems unlikely that the choice of name—Diana—was coincidental; how apt to choose the goddess of the hunt who was averse to a marriage.
4. *The Years Between*, Daphne du Maurier.

Women want love to be a novel, men a short story.
—Daphne du Maurier

The Office
by María Irene Fornés

Directed by **Alice Reagan**
Dramaturgy by **Morgan Jenness**

Wednesday, October 1, 2014

Visionary Irene by Andrea Lepcio

MARÍA IRENE FORNÉS is a pivotal figure in Hispanic-American and experimental theatre, both for her unique vision as a writer and for her dedication as a director and teacher. She emigrated to the United States from Cuba at the age of 14, with her mother and sister, after her father died. At 19, she became interested in painting and began her formal education in abstract art, studying with artist Hans Hofmann in New York City and Provincetown, Massachusetts. In 1954, she moved to Paris to study painting. There, she was inspired to write plays after seeing Samuel Beckett's *Waiting for Godot*. She said in a 2002 interview,

> "He was very gloomy but he had a great sense of humor. He had the whole audience laughing." She added, "When I saw Beckett, I thought, 'why did I have to see this to think I could do it?'"

She returned to New York in 1957. Her first play was *The Widow* (1961) followed by *There! You Died* (later re-titled *Tango Palace*) which was first produced by San Francisco's Actors Workshop in 1963 and then at New York City's Actors Studio in 1964. This play established Fornés' theatrical production style, in which she was involved in the entire staging process. The musical comedy *Promenade* followed in 1965 with book and lyrics by Fornés and music by Rev. Al Carmines. It ran for three weekends at Judson Memorial Church, winning an Obie before transferring to a commercial run off-Broadway at the Promenade Theatre (named for the play) in 1969. The cast was led by Madeline Kahn.

Other plays include *The Office* (1966), *A Vietnamese Wedding* (1967), *Dr. Kheal, Molly's Dream* (1968) and then came her most recognized work, *Fefu and Her Friends* (1977). In *Fefu*, Irene deconstructs the familiar stage, removing the fourth wall and staging scenes in multiple locations simultaneously throughout the theater. The audience is divided into groups to watch each scene, then they rotate to the next set, as the scene is repeated until each group has seen all scenes. First produced by the New York Theater Strategy at the Relativity Media Lab, the story concerns eight women who, on the surface, appear to be engaging in mishaps with men, and it climaxes in a murder scene. It is a feminist play that focuses on female characters and their thoughts, feelings and interrelationships and is told from a woman's perspective.

She subsequently wrote *Evelyn Brown* (1980), *The Danube* (1982), *Mud* (1983) and the Obie-winning *Sarita* (1984). *The Conduct of Life* (1985) was another Obie winner, as was *Abingdon Square* (1988); she was also a finalist for the 1990 Pulitzer Prize with her play *And What of the Night?*. *Enter the Night* was written in 1993, but did not receive its New York Premiere until 2000.

From 1973-79, Fornés was the managing director of the New York Theatre Strategy. Besides directing most of her own plays, as well as plays by Calderon, Ibsen, Chekhov and several contemporary authors. Fornés has had a long collaboration with INTAR Theatre in New York City where she created the Hispanic Playwrights-in-Residence Laboratory in 1981 to nurture the work of Latino theatre artists.

As a teacher, she pulled from her background as a visual artist, encouraging students to sketch characters to get into their work. Classes would start with yoga and other physical activities. She urged students to trust their characters, follow where they led and not to try to impose plot or action on them. Students were asked to read their own work and Fornés would instruct them not to act, to simply say the words, believing that truth and any falseness would be revealed. As a teacher, she was honest and always excited about the work.

Two volumes of her plays have been published by the *17* and other plays have appeared in various anthologies. She completed a TCG/PEW Artist-in-Residence at Women's Project and Productions. The 1999-2000 season at Signature Theatre Company was devoted to the Fornés oeuvre, which included the world premiere of her latest play *Letters From Cuba*. It focuses on a young female Cuban dancer living in New York who corresponds with her brother back home. The play is the first that Fornés identified as being drawn from her own personal experience of nearly 30 years of letter writing with her brother. It earned her another Obie.

In all, Fornés wrote more than 40 stage works, received nine Obie Awards for both writing and directing her plays, and received a Guggenheim Fellowship. Her work continues to be performed around the world, both professionally and at many universities and colleges. Fornés now lives in a New York City senior home where she is visited regularly by her many colleagues and students.

A Different Type Of Work
by Morgan Jenness

The Office is a play that has become somewhat mythologized. Many people are surprised that Maria Irene Fornés actually holds the title of being the first Off-Off Broadway playwright to have been produced *on* Broadway. Some people will have never heard of the play until tonight. Some may have heard but know very little of it. Few people have read it, or experienced it directly. I myself only learned of it when Patrick Herold and I blessedly inherited Fornés' body of work as literary agents, upon the passing of Irene's long-time agent Helen Merrill, but there didn't seem to be a script in the computer or in the files at the agency and Irene didn't seem to know if she did indeed have a copy somewhere, nor did she seem to have too much concern about it. It seemed to be an event in her career for which she had a kind of bemused pride, though not enough interest to try to revisit.

Sometime later, when it became clear that Irene's health would not allow her to live alone in her West Village apartment, as playwright Eduardo Machado and I were packing up her files to move to safekeeping, we discovered an elegant maroon bound script, with a title page that identified it as the property of producer Harold Prince. It was indeed a long lost copy of *The Office*, and it seemed that Mr. Prince had perhaps been considering becoming involved because of his relationship with its director Jerome Robbins—though we never managed to ferret out the entire story.

The person who seems to have the most information about the play's past is esteemed scholar, writer, and long time friend to Irene, Scott T. Cummings—who talks about it in his book MARIA IRENE FORNÉS, which I am excerpting here:

"While Fornés was a member of the Playwrights Unit of the Actors Studio, portions of the comedy she was writing called *The Office* were workshopped there. The Establishment Theatre Company, led by movie mogul Joseph E. Levine, the anti-establishment British comedian Peter Cook, and the Off-Broadway producer Ivor David Balding, acquired the rights to the unfinished play and hired director/choreographer Jerome Robbins, fresh off the success of his *Fiddler On The Roof*, to stage the play on Broadway. Robbins, most renowned for his ballet and Broadway musical work, had also directed Arthur Kopit's black comedy *Oh, Dad, Poor Dad, Mama's Hung You In The Closet And I'm Feelin' So Sad* for the Phoenix Theatre in 1962 and Brecht's *Mother Courage And Her Children*, starring Anne Bancroft, on Broadway in 1963. For Fornés, it was an early, sudden and short-lived leap into the commercial mainstream.

The Office takes place around Christmastime in the offices of Hinch, Inc., a shipping company in sharp decline since the recent death of its founder. The action centers on the bumbling, neurotic office manager Albert Pfancoo, who hopes to lead the business back to prosperity. He is beleaguered by three comic female figures: Princess, Hinch's plump, sensuous widow; Miss Punk, a strait-laced spinster secretary who refuses to be fired; and Shirley Bisbee, the misfit girl-Friday he wants to hire in her stead. The comedy takes a strange, magical turn when it turns out that a portrait of the late, lamented George Hinch can talk and soon confesses love for Shirley."

(I won't give things away but the portrait can do more than talk.)

The Office was scheduled to open at Henry Miller's Theater on May 12, 1966 with a cast that included Elaine May (Shirley), Jack Weston (Pfancoo), Ruth White (Princess) and Doris Roberts (Miss Punk). But the producers seemed to grow nervous about negative reviews and closed the show after ten preview performances. Clive Barnes would later refer to *The Office* as "a New York evening that never officially opened, but is well-spoken of by a loyal preview public," but Fornés never returned to Broadway or, it seems, to the play.

An interesting footnote to the story is a 2000 *New York Times* panel interview with four playwrights (Arthur Miller, Edward Albee, Horton Foote and John Guare) who, along with Irene, were each having a full season of their work produced by the visionary Signature Theater Company. The panel started to talk about some of the challenges the various writers had faced and John Guare referenced Irene's "very, very bad experience in the commercial world" 34 years earlier—which had perhaps seemed to marginalize her work somewhat—to which Fornés responded:

> "I am in some ways, lucky that I'm not as successful or well known as the gentlemen who are with me here. What I mean by that is simply my work is not done on Broadway. My work is more Off-Off Broadway...not even Off-Broadway...it's almost like a different type of work" ("Reunion": ARS)

As long as I have known her, María Irene Fornés has had a strong sense of her own different type of work, and also a sense that the path in which she was always the most interested, was the one which would best serve the work itself.

I am thrilled that we all are having the opportunity to be on that path tonight.

I know everything. Half of it I really know. The Rest I Make Up.

—María Irene Fornés

"Women on the Verge"
Overtones and *Fourteen*
by Alice Erya Gerstenberg

Directed by **Melissa Attebery**
Dramaturgy by **Mari Lyn Henry**
Assistant Director: **India Van Camp**

Wednesday, September 23, 2015

Alice (Erya) Gerstenberg **by Mari Lyn Henry**

Descended from the House of Gerstenberg, grain merchants who founded the Chicago Board of Trade, Alice was the only child of Julia, a woman with no formal education who had had aspirations of becoming an actress and Erich, a successful businessman. She enjoyed a lifestyle available only to the very wealthy. After being enrolled at a private school in Chicago, her mother decided she should attend Bryn Mawr. Founded in 1885, Bryn Mawr was a women's liberal arts college based on Quaker values. The curriculum offered women a more progressive academic program than any others, and it prepared them for meaningful opportunities to contribute to the world so they could compete with men.

In 1908, a year after her graduation, she began writing plays professionally. *A Little World* contained four one-acts written for girls in a Chicago acting school. She also published two feminist novels which were highly successful. *Unquenched Fire* (1912) concerns Jane, a Chicago society girl who goes to New York to be an actress. She is aware of her ability to be in an emotional situation while at the same time able to watch and chart her own reactions and those of others. Jane embodies the split between woman and artist and in the end must choose between them. In her memoirs, Alice wrote of a similar ability of consciously filing serious or funny moments away for future use in her work. She was already employing the split subject in her themes.

Overtones (1913) her most well-known and still oft-produced one-act about the primitive vs. the cultured selves of two women, was inspired by a visit to an acquaintance from Chicago who had moved to Manhattan. The friend asked her husband twice within a few seconds whether, as he left to visit a neighbor, he was going to take the car. At this point, Alice reminisced "I heard a click at the top of my head, as if the shutter of a camera had closed and my mind said to me about her, 'I know you have an automobile, I heard you the first time." We are not two women sitting on this couch having tea. We are four women, each with an underlying self." Feminist objectives recur in her novels and plays and reflect her interest in the inner psyche as "a critique of a society that represses women so severely they break apart."

Two years after the publication of Freud's *The Interpretation of Dreams*, she was the first playwright to give Broadway an authentic glimpse into unconscious life. *Overtones* was produced by the Washington Square Players with a set designed by Lee Simonson in 1915 and performed in repertory with other short plays at the Bandbox Theatre (E. 57th St. and 3rd Ave.) until May 1916. After its run there, it toured on Martin Beck's Vaudeville circuit, performed at the Palace Theatre in Chicago and in London where Lillie Langtry starred as Harriet.

Interviewed for a New York daily in 1915, she was described as a "little, blond-haired, blue-eyed schoolgirl...perched on the arm of a chair with a letter from her daddy." She was actually 30 and had just published her second novel, *The Conscience of Sarah Platt*, and was already known for her successful stage adaptation of *Alice in Wonderland*.

What is easy to describe in novels, such as unrealistic distortions of space, swift transitions, long falls down holes and flying through the air, was, to say the least, challenging when compressing the action of two novels into a comprehensible play; lighting, set design, music and stage directions were daunting. In Gerstenberg's adaptation, when Alice escapes from the Red Queen the stage direction involved her jumping over "the footlights on the bridge and as the curtain falls dividing her from the crowd, she appeals to the audience to save her." This is one of the first examples of a character breaking through the proscenium and engaging in direct address to the audience in the American theatre. One critic noted that nearly thirty playwrights had tried unsuccessfully to dramatize Carroll's stories and "it remained for Alice Gerstenberg to dramatize the book successfully as Carroll wanted it."

The story of the psychological maturing of the American drama is connected to the emergence of the Art Theatre or Little Theatre movement, which led the revolt against the hackneyed commercial theatre in New York referred to as the Great "Trite" Way. Between 1912 and 1915 Little Theatres sprang up in various parts of the country including Chicago, Detroit, Baltimore, Provincetown, and the Neighborhood Playhouse and Washington Square Players in New York.

Gerstenberg was a pioneer in the movement and one of the original members of the Chicago Little Theatre founded by Maurice Browne in 1912. She and Annette Washburne started the Chicago Junior League for Children in 1921. Her most significant contribution to the theatre was in being founder, producer and president of The Playwrights' Theatre of Chicago (1922-1945).[1]

Her plays and investment in the community embraced her concerns for fellowship, self-expression and anti-commercialism that the Little Theatre movement fought for. She believed that it was "necessary for a woman to be a human being first and a woman afterward and to learn to express her individuality with the same freedom and confidence that men do!" But her feminism is too easily lost in critiques of her work that see only the upper-class milieus or the satirized women's behavior. While her characters like Mrs. Pringle in *Fourteen*, or Lois in *The Unseen* are often frivolous or shallow, she also wrote about women of substance like the psychic Grace in *Attuned* or Miss Ivory, the savvy ingénue in her updated restoration farce *The Pot Boiler* who outsmarts Sud, the inept playwright.

She was often urged to move to New York, but preferred to remain in Chicago tending to her supportive parents and stating, "Chicago's climate itself stimulates the "I will" spirit. We kept on striving to build for a richer soil in the arts."

Described in an early interview as a 'girl author', she rebutted with "There should be no condemning laws for women and condoning laws for men. There should be but one law for both, and that a clean, broad, uplifting, developing human law, a law of honest self-expression." She never married but chose to devote her life entirely to the theatre and to improving the lives of women, practicing what she preached most passionately and eloquently.

---

1. According to The Newberry Research Library, Chicago, which houses the Alice Gerstenberg papers, 1903-1971.

Alice in Chicagoland by Mari Lyn Henry

Gerstenberg's fellow Bryn Mawr alumna, producer Theresa Helburn, Class of 1909, wrote: "I smile when I think of the rather priggish morality and unsuspected conventionality with which we condemned the double standard and upheld free love with a rather humorless determination to back good causes and generally enlighten the world."

It was a restless time, values were being questioned, dozens of new schools and movements in art were erupting. Cubism was duking it out with futurism and everybody wrote free verse. The International Exhibition of Art (1913) had brought modern art to America and a new set of books had appeared including Theodore Dreiser's controversial *Sister Carrie* (1900), Edgar Lee Masters' *Spoon River Anthology* (1915) demystifying rural America, and Ernest Poole's *The Harbor* (1915) advocating for the unionization of dock workers.

"Little Theatres," begun in Chicago in 1912 had sprung up around the country in opposition to the stifling hand of the commercial Theatre Syndicate. They began writing and producing their own plays, experimenting with new forms of storytelling, acting styles, dialogue and mise-en-scène to suit the times. The development of the Provincetown Players in 1915, led by Susan Glaspell and George Cram Cook, set the standard for the passionate conviction that theatre should be a medium of serious artistic expression of important issues and not just a money-grubbing enterprise. In that same year and "because *everyone* seemed to be writing one-act plays," Lawrence Langner inaugurated informal evenings of play readings which became the Washington Square Players, named after the Boni Brothers' bookshop on Washington Square Park where the plan had been conceived. (Langner would go on to create the Theatre Guild with Helburn in 1918, which still exists today.)

In Greenwich Village, psychoanalysis was an intriguing new fad. Glaspell and Cook's play *Suppressed Desires* dealt with Freudianism in America, satirizing the effects of the principal character's obsession with psychoanalysis and her adoration of the doctor, which almost destroys her marriage. It was reported that the intellectuals would "rather 'psych' each other than eat." There was such fascination with the new lingo about the libido, the id, and the super ego that Ms. Glaspell exclaimed: "You could not buy a bun without hearing of someone's complex!"

It was in this forward moving group that Gerstenberg found her first success as a playwright. She could be labeled a Bohemian artist or a Greenwich Village feminist but labels bothered her. What she had in common with this group was probing the psyche of her characters in new forms that would express the troubled spirit of the modern woman. *Overtones* is thought to be the first American play to depart from realism and to show the unconscious self.[1]

Eugene O'Neill, who had undergone psychoanalysis in 1927, clearly was influenced by Gerstenberg. In *Strange Interlude* he uses "thought asides" similar to her split protagonist; others referred to them as interior monologues. Audiences were impressed; his play ran for 426 performances and won the Pulitzer. He is considered "the founder of a new dramatic form equal to the challenge of modern psychology, restoring insight into the tragic outcomes of human motives."[2] Today, most people have never heard of Gerstenberg.

But Gerstenberg was, in fact, known nationwide on the Vaudeville circuit, the most popular form of indigenous entertainment between 1893 and 1925. One-act plays lent dignity to the bill of entertainment and she had many of them. *Overtones* was presented at Chicago's Palace Theatre by Martin Beck, founder of the Orpheum Circuit. *The Pot Boiler* was presented not only in Vaudeville, but in a trench in France, in Hawaii, as well as little theatres in Chicago, New York, San Francisco and Hollywood. Her inventive last line for this modern Restoration farce cleverly turns the lens upon herself. When the character of the playwright doesn't know how to end his absurd playlet. "I don't know who shoots!" he shrieks (in Vaudeville the ingénue traditionally asked, "Who Shoots?") Gerstenberg's players exclaim in disgust, "Oh, shoot the author!"

Fourteen is a one-act social satire originally performed at Maitland's Theatre in San Francisco in 1919 and published in the February 1920 issue of *The Drama* magazine, in which J. Vandervoort Sloan described Gerstenberg as "a progressive young playwright, possibly the best-known and most widely be-played by amateur groups in America" and *Fourteen* as belonging "in the 'A' class of her plays." A reviewer for the American Library Association called it an "exemplary social farce" and it continues to be produced to this day. The character of Mrs. Pringle foreshadows Hyacinth Bouquet in the British sitcom *Keeping Up Appearances* and Billie Burke's social climbing hostess in *Dinner At Eight* (I suspect Edna Ferber had seen a performance of *Fourteen*.)

Gerstenberg's Midwest origins put her in association not only with Iowa's Susan Glaspell, but also Wisconsin's Zona Gale and Missouri's Zoe Akins. She was dedicated to the Chicago Little Theatre movement and was passionately invested in creating production opportunities for authors who remained outside of New York, serving on the board of the Society of Midland Authors. This quote in praise of the founder John M. Stahl gives a sense of that dedication, the resistance the society encountered, and Gerstenberg's frank but literary turn of phrase: "*Some people were aggravated by his eagerness to make a success of this society. Most people never even try to exercise the second commandment, they are so busy looking at the outside of a fellow without taking an accompanying glance at the inner soul. I admire people who have the initiative to put something worthwhile into the world as against those who remain lumps of criticism in the path.*"

She embraced spiritualism and its emphasis on freedom of conscience. It became a magnet for social radicals, especially advocates of women's rights and abolition. They sought knowledge of the world beyond. Alice tackled this subject matter in her one act monologue *Beyond* about a dead woman awaiting judgment from the All Powerful.

Scholar Dorothy Chansky, author of *Composing Ourselves: The Little Theatre Movement and the American Audience*, summarizes Gerstenberg's contributions as follows: "She greeted changes with a willingness to go on writing, producing, and speaking about and on behalf of women and theatre. Her life was transitional in the sense that she made, rather than resisted changes. If she was unwilling or unable to play the role of the tough rebel or to give up her financial status, she accomplished for decades the feat that was often short-lived for female playwrights of the Progressive Era. Alice the artist and Alice the woman continued to face each other in the mirror. One can imagine they were often smiling."

---

1. Sievers, W. David. *Freud on Broadway: A History of Psychoanalysis and the American Drama*. Hermitage House. 1955.
2. Ibid.

I admire people who have the initiative to put something worthwhile into the world against those who remain lumps of criticism in the path.

—Alice Erya Gerstenberg

The Verge
by Susan Glaspell

Directed by **Melissa Attebery**
Dramaturgy by **Andrea Lepcio**

Monday, August 12, 2013

Susan Glaspell: Player, Playwright, Pioneer
by Andrea Lepcio

Susan Keating Glaspell (1876-1948) was born in Davenport, Iowa. She appears to have never been held back by expectations for female behavior, doing well in school and by the age of 18 working as a journalist for the local paper. She went on to college at Drake University to earn a degree in Philosophy. After graduating, she went to work as a reporter for the *Des Moines Daily News*, assigned to the State legislature and murder cases. This type of assignment was rare for a women in her day. Her first play, *Trifles*, was based on a murder trial she covered while a reporter. Having already sold some short stories, she returned to Davenport to write more short stories and novels. Her first novel, *The Glory of the Conquered*, came out in 1909.

She met and fell in love with George Cram Cook who was married. They had an affair and eventually married in 1913. The scandal encouraged them to move East where they spent summers in Provincetown and winters in New York City. In Greenwich Village, Glaspell was a founder and member of Heterodoxy, a radical group of women activists. Together with friends, they formed the Provincetown Players. The Players was part of the Little Theater movement that emerged around 1912 in response both to the commercialism of Broadway and the emergence of motion pictures. It aimed, according to its current website, to "give venue to American playwrights and new American plays, purposefully encouraging plays that would be in contrast to the melo-dramas and triangle relationship plays they observed producers were presenting on Broadway."

Glaspell and Cook discovered Eugene O'Neill and invited him into the group. After a couple of seasons on Cape Cod, the theater moved to 133 MacDougal Street. The story goes that it was Cook who simply announced that his wife was going to write a play. They had already written one together, but in the 1916 season she contributed *Trifles*. She went on to write 11 plays that were all produced by the Players. Her plays range from realism to expressionistic. Critics did not always understand or support her work, but she was respected. In 1922, after *The* Verge (1921), critic Ludwig Lewisohn wrote "This power of creating human speech which shall be at once concrete and significant, convincing in detail and spiritually cumulative in progression is, of course, the essential gift of the authentic dramatist. That gift Miss Glaspell always possessed in measure; she has now brought it to a rich and effective maturity."

By 1922, the success of *Emperor Jones* and associated disagreements over becoming too commercial, led Glaspell and Cook to leave the Provincetown Players and move to Greece where Cook died in 1924. Glaspell returned to Provincetown, writing more novels and a biography of her husband. *Brook Evans* was made into a film by Paramount Pictures with a screenplay by Zöe Akins, under the title *The Right to Love*. In 1931, she won the Pulitzer Prize for *Alison's House* performed by Eva Le Gallienne's Civic Repertory Theatre. During the Depression, she served as director of the Midwest Play Bureau and was instrumental in the development of the Living Newspapers. She spent her remaining years in Provincetown writing four more novels.

Glaspell was highly regarded as a novelist and dramatist during her time. Towards the end of her life, how-ever, a new generation of Broadway critics wrote against her work and after her death her novels fell out of print. In the 1970s, the re-emergence of feminism contributed to renewed interest in her writing. Today there is significant scholarship on her plays and novels and much of her work is back in print. In 2003, the International Susan Glaspell Society was founded.

Glaspell's writing bridged the Victorian and modern eras, tracking women's emerging freedom and self-defini-tion within a changing but ever patriarchal society. She was a keen observer, in particular, of women's relation-ships with each other as friends and sisters, mothers and daughters. In both content and form, she stretched boundaries and experimented. Ultimately, her work is universal in its exploration of the individual and society, American identity, the impact of war, the demands of marriage and the meaning and purpose of life.

The Verge: An Exquisite Expression of Expressionism
by Andrea Lepcio

Any research on *The Verge* will immediately confirm that it is an "Expressionist Play." Unfortunately, if one then looks up "Expressionist Drama," only O'Neill, Rice and other plays by men are mentioned...and sometimes Sophie Treadwell's *Machinal*. This is the quintessential reason for On Her Shoulders! Susan Glaspell's play is a remarkable drama in its storytelling, its use of symbolism and expressionist methods, and in its theatricality. Mardi Valgemae notes the play "was the first American play to be qualified as expressionistic." The last of the series of plays that Glaspell wrote for the Provincetown Players, *The Verge* is the most avant-garde and modernist. C. W. E. Bigsby writes Glaspell attempts "a radical revisioning of all aspects of theatre" that "few writers, before or since have dared."

Expressionism originated in Germany and was first applied to poetry and painting. Expressionists are interested in conveying how the world *feels* subjectively rather than how it is *perceived to be* objectively. The movement began before the First World War and continued through to the Weimar Republic, expanding the form to literature, dance, architecture, music, theater and film. Plays in this style are referred to as Stationendramen (station dramas) which is a reference to Christ's Stations of the Cross. In *The Verge*, we experience Claire (the protagonist) laboring through a series of obstacles toward her ultimate objective and action. Language is heightened as characters struggle against societal values and authority. CLAIRE: *"I want to break it up! I tell you, I want to break it up! If it were all in pieces, we'd be shocked to aliveness, wouldn't we? There would be strange new comings together—mad new comings together, and we would know what it is to be born, and then we might know—that we are. Smash it. As you'd smash an egg."* And she does. Violence erupts in waves in *The Verge*.

Sets, too convey the sense of something awry—they are stark, distorted, angled and extraordinary. The play opens in a greenhouse in winter, and Act III returns there. For the second act, we climb to *"...a tower which is thought to be round but does not complete the circle. The back is curved, then jagged lines break from that, and the front is a queer bulging window—in a curve that leans. The whole structure is as if given a twist by some terrific force—like something wrong...A delicately distorted rail of a spiral staircase winds up from an opening in the floor below."*

The Verge and other expressionist plays came after the horror that was World War I or, as it was called at the time, the Great War (July 1914-November 1918). Of the 60 million European soldiers mobilized, 8 million were killed, 7 million disabled and 15 million injured. The U.S. didn't enter the war until 1918, but beginning that summer it sent 10,000 soldiers each day to France; as a result of the delay in entering the war only 117,000 American lives were lost. Thus, changes brought by the war were more immediate, painful and life-changing in Europe. But, from a distance, Americans were aware of the devastation and the impact of the demise of four empires: German, Austro-Hungarian, Ottoman and Russian.

For all involved then, life was forever changed in ways it would take time to understand. Glaspell's reflections on the war, from an American perspective, are fascinating. On the one hand, Claire's daughter, Elizabeth, feels the war has freed them to pursue life and be productive—it is an opportunity for rebirth.

> ELIZABETH: "It was the war, wasn't it, made it the thing to do something." She goes on that her teacher has instructed her that "We should each do some expressive thing—you know what I mean? And that this is the keynote of the age. Of course, one's own kind of thing. Like mother—growing flowers."

Claire expresses quite the opposite view.

> CLAIRE: "it was a stunning chance! But fast as we could—scuttled right back to the trim little thing we'd been shocked out of." She goes on: "—a stunning chance! Mankind massed to kill. We have failed. We are through. We will destroy. Break this up—it can't go farther. In the air above—in the sea below—it is to kill! All we had thought we were—we aren't. We were shut in with what wasn't so. Is there one ounce of energy has not gone to this killing? Is there one love not torn in two? Throw it in! Now? Ready? Break up. Push. Harder. Break up. And then—and then—"

Be the most that you can be, so life will be more because you were.
—Susan Glaspell

Diana of Dobson's
by Cecily Hamilton

Directed by **Gwynn MacDonald**
Dramaturgy by **Loren Noveck**
New Adaptation by **Susan Jonas**

Monday, July 15, 2013

Cicely Hamilton: Actress, Playwright, Journalist, Feminist, Suffragist **by Loren Noveck**

Cicely Hamilton (1872–1952) came to writing as a profession more than an artistic calling, a means to support herself and her sister. Her published output includes six full-length plays, three one-acts, seven novels (three also published as plays, including *Diana of Dobson's*), seventeen nonfiction books (including perhaps her most famous work, *Marriage as a Trade*, and a nine-book series on modern Europe from 1931 to 1950), and countless articles, pamphlets, and speeches. (Ten more plays were never published, though most of them were produced.) For her whole career, her writing went side by side with political and social activism, which might be seen as her genuine passion (and, of course, comes through in her writing; in *Diana of Dobson's*, the political issues include rights of working women, the pay scales of shopgirls, and one of her common themes, the economics of marriage).

Hamilton was born in 1872, as Cicely Mary Hammill, the oldest of four children. Before she was twenty, both her parents had passed away, both her brothers had been shipped off to Canada to make their own ways in the world, and her sister, Evelyn, was trying to become a governess. Cicely started her self-supporting life as a "pupil-teacher" (something sort of like a modern teaching assistant, who pays tuition by giving lessons to other students), but (in her own words) she turned her "back on the teaching profession before it turned its back on me." Instead, she decided to become an actress, changing her name to Hamilton and working primarily with the lowest rung of touring companies.

By 1903, she'd tired of the touring circuit and, now needing to support her sister, returned to London and began writing.

Although she had aspirations as a playwright, it proved more lucrative to begin with romantic fiction and sensation stories for pulp periodicals. Her first play was produced in London and Brighton in 1906; at the advice of the producer she disguised her name to hide her sex. Hamilton credits the suffrage movement—with which she was about to become involved—with the subsequent decision to put her full name on everything else she ever wrote. Spurred by her own varied work experiences and the need to support herself and her sister, Hamilton was intensely committed to making sure women had the means to obtain financial security and, for lack of a historically appropriate term, self-esteem. Suffragism was an important part of this project, but only a part: "My personal revolt was feminist rather than suffragist." Her important work *Marriage as a Trade* (1909) was concerned with women's financial self-sufficiency, rather than their political emancipation, and how that factored into the marriage contract and their ability to choose to marry or not and whom.

By then, Hamilton was active in the suffrage campaign, helping to found the Women Writers' Suffrage League and the Actresses' Franchise League in 1908.

Even after the beginning of women's enfranchisement in Britain, Hamilton remained active, politically and artistically. She continued to write plays, columns, novels; edit the League for European Freedom's press bulletins; and give speeches until the end of her life.

Major works, in addition to *Diana*, include the plays (several of which were also published as novels) *Just to Get Married*, *The Cutting of the Knot* (also known as *A Matter of Money*), *Jack and Jill and a Friend*, *Lady Noggs*, and *The Old Adam*; the novels *William, an Englishman*, *Theodore Savage*, and *Full Stop*; and the nonfiction works *Marriage as a Trade*, *Senlis*, her autobiography *Life Errant*, *Lament for Democracy*, and *The Englishwoman*.

Diana of Dobson's and the Economics of Womanhood
by Loren Noveck

Diana of Dobson's was Cicely Hamilton's first full-length play and the second production by Lena Ashwell's Kingsway Theatre, in February 1908. Said the theater's reader, Edward Knoblock, "Just about five in a hundred were worth reading at all...one in two hundred ready to put on stage with a fair chance of success." Knoblock saw *Diana's* potential right away: its strong characters; its humor; its passionate explication of ideas.

As a woman who had to support herself from a young age, and never married, Cicely Hamilton—who worked as a teacher and an actress before finding success as a writer—had an exquisite awareness of both the power and freedom bought by money, and the constraints placed by social mores on women's ability to acquire that power and freedom. And although she could not have, obviously, used the term, what strikes me as relevant about *Diana of Dobson's* is that it's very much about the contemporary issue of income inequality, here operating intertwined with both class and gender.

For Diana Massingberd, Hamilton's heroine, it is impossible not to think, constantly, about the vast gulfs that exist between her position behind the counter in a drapery shop—selling goods she can't dream of affording and living in a grim dormitory—and the plutocrat (the "one-percenter," to use today's term) who owns that store; it's impossible not to think of how few options she has when, unlike her coworker Kitty, she sees no prospect of marriage, the only path likely, in that time and place, to get her off the lowest rung of paid work. (Her path, of course, takes her past several possible marriages by the end of the play, but none of these are predictable at the beginning.) It's telling that the play is called *Diana of Dobson's*, not *Diana Massingberd*; her life at the start of the play is so constrained by that place of employment that it dictates everything for her.

Diana's unexpected inheritance, then, allows her to be, albeit briefly, Massingberd rather than "of Dobson's." Three hundred pounds, which she spends on a brief period of luxury rather than improving her lot incrementally over a longer period, represents 23 years of her salary. (For today's minimum-wage worker, this would be like inheriting around $200,000; not enough to change your life in a permanent way unless you're extremely frugal, but if you were going to blow it all in a month, you could live in the lap of considerable luxury—and of course in Hamilton's era there was no minimum wage and very few worker protection laws, so the contrast in lifestyles was even more extreme.) Even the money Diana does end up marrying is a vast improvement on her current lot. If she was momentarily living the life of someone with 276 times her income, "settling" for 46 times isn't really so bad.

Yet as one goes up the play's economic ladder—from the shopgirls to the moneyed tourists in the Swiss Alps—every character in it, except for perhaps the plutocrat Sir Jabez Grinley, is conscious not just of their relative social position, but of exactly how much money is required to keep or improve it. As members of society's non-working classes, women like Mrs. Cantelupe or young men-about-town like Victor Bretherton see money as a thing one can acquire by a method almost entirely unrelated to how one spends one's time. It's only when forced to attempt to earn income by his own labor that Victor comes to think of his small fortune as riches indeed.

As a purportedly rich widow, observed in conspicuous consumption, Diana is putting on a masquerade not only of class (though of course it is that), and not only of a particular gendered status (marriage), but of unconcern with money, of having enough money not to think about money, which, ironically, is what makes her attractive to Sir Jabez. Unlike Sir Jabez Grinley, for a woman it's not enough to have "grit and push and pluck enough to raise [one]self out of the ruck and finish at the top"; Diana has all those qualities in spades, but they get her docked wages rather than success. Nonetheless, she is enormously—and rightly—proud of herself for earning her bread, for making her way in the world "without being beholden to any man and without a penny at my back."

That position, and that sense of pride, are very much Hamilton's own; it was crucially important to her that women be able to find their place in society outside of marriage, outside of being dependent on even the most beloved of husbands. As she writes in *Marriage as a Trade*, "I hold...that the narrowing down of woman's hopes and ambitions to the sole pursuit and sphere of marriage is one of the principal causes of the various disabilities, economic and otherwise, under which she labors today. And I hold, also, that this concentration of all her hopes and ambitions on the one object was, to a great extent, the result of artificial pressure, of unsound economic and social conditions—conditions which forced her energy into one channel, by the simple expedient of depriving it of every other outlet, and made marriage practically compulsory."

It's somewhat bittersweet, then, to realize that despite Hamilton's political commitments and Diana's fiery spirit, this play (like many of Hamilton's plays) ends with that most conventional comedic wrap-up: a marriage. Are we meant to see this as, in the end, a pragmatic and financially prudent decision, or a genuine romance—between characters who almost never interact in the play? Are we meant to be happy for Diana because her days of penury are over, or because she's genuinely attached to Victor—or are we meant, just a little, to be worried for the freedom she's giving up?

> *By a woman, then, I understand an individual human being whose life is her own concern; whose worth, in my eyes . . . is in no way advanced or detracted from by the accident of marriage . . .*
>
> —Cicely Hamilton

Les Blancs
by Lorraine Hansberry

Directed by **Pat Golden**
Dramaturgy by **Andrea Lepcio**

Monday, October 21, 2013

Lorraine Hansberry: "Sighted Eyes and a Feeling Heart"
by Andrea Lepcio

"I was born black and female," said Lorraine Hansberry the youngest American playwright, the fifth woman, and the only black writer to ever win the New York Drama Critics Circle Award for Best Play of the Year. Speaking to the winners of a United Negro College Fund writing contest she continued, "I say all of this to say that one cannot live with sighted eyes and feeling heart and not know and react to the miseries which afflict this world." She would spend her all too brief life writing—plays, essays, articles, poetry—in reaction to what she saw and how she felt about it.

Lorraine Hansberry was born and raised in Chicago where her father fought all the way to the Supreme Court to defend his purchase of a home in a white neighborhood—which would inspire her first and most well-known play, *A Raisin in the Sun*. She attended the University of Wisconsin for two years, growing in political activism before moving to New York in 1950 to became a reporter for Paul Robeson's newspaper, *Freedom* and then Associate Editor. In that capacity she attended the Intercontinental Peace Congress in Montevideo, Uruguay, in 1952, when Robeson was denied a passport to attend. She also took classes on Africa with W. E.B. Dubois.

She met Robert Nemiroff, a Jewish publisher, songwriter and political activist on a picket line, and they were married in 1953, spending the night before their wedding protesting the execution of the Rosenbergs. Moving with her husband to Croton-on-Hudson, Lorraine Hansberry continued not only her writing but also her involvement with civil rights and other political protest.

As she began to write plays, Hansberry recalled that she had seen a rehearsal of Sean O'Casey's *Juno and the Paycock* in college, about which she would later write, "One of the sound ideas of dramatic writing is that in order to create the universal, you must pay very great attention to the specific." Her plays certainly reflect this point of view. She did not believe in art for art's sake and believed that all plays make a social statement.

Raisin in the Sun was completed in 1957 and debuted in 1959, the first play by an African-American woman on Broadway. She was only 29 years old. After the success of the play (and subsequent film version) Hansberry was commissioned to write a television drama on slavery, which she completed as *The Drinking Gourd,* but it was not produced. NBC executives apparently didn't support the idea of a black screenwriter writing about slavery.

Her marriage lasted only six years but the working relationship continued; Hansberry subsequently dated both men and women and joined the lesbian-feminist organization Daughters of Biliis. She wrote letters to the editor using only her initials explaining " . . . homosexual persecution and condemnation has at its roots not only social ignorance, but a philosophically active anti-feminist dogma."

During her lifetime many of her essays and articles were published. In 1964, *The Movement: Documentary of a Struggle for Equality* was published for SNCC (Southern Nonviolent Coordinating Committee), with text by Hansberry. Her only other play to receive a Broadway production while she was alive was *The Sign in Sidney Brustein's Window*, which played for 101 performances and closed the night she died. She had become ill with pancreatic cancer during the production and as she was writing *Les Blancs*. Upon her death, James Baldwin, referring to her clear-eyed view of the world and its troubles wrote, "it is not at all farfetched to suspect that what she saw contributed to the strain which killed her, for the effort to which Lorraine was dedicated is more than enough to kill a man."

Her ex-husband, Robert Nemiroff, became the executor for several unfinished manuscripts. He added minor changes to complete the play *Les Blancs* which Julius Lester termed her best work, and he adapted many of her writings into the play *To Be Young, Gifted and Black*, which was the longest-running Off Broadway play of the 1968-1969 season. It appeared in book form the following year under the title, *To Be Young, Gifted and Black: Lorraine Hansberry in Her Own Words*. At Lorraine's funeral, a message from Dr. Martin Luther King, Jr. predicted: "her creative ability and her profound grasp of the deep social issues confronting the world today will remain an inspiration to generations yet unborn." That promise is still being fulfilled today.

The Quest for Freedom in Hansberry's *Les Blancs*
by Andrea Lepcio

Les Blancs was the first major work by a black American playwright to criticize colonialism and address the African liberation struggle, while openly questioning whether or not freedom could be won without violence. To do so, Hansberry created complex, diverse characters representing multiple aspects of White and Black experience. She opens in a scene at the crude Mission hospital introducing us to doctors doing their best under the leadership of an absent Reverend. The Reverend, his wife and doctors have committed their lives to helping the people of the imaginary country of Zatembe (believed to be a stand in for Kenya), but have purposefully chosen to keep the means of that help rudimentary, relative to the more sophisticated care available in nearby hospitals for Whites. The character of the Reverend, who never appears, was modeled, according to Steven Carter (University of Puerto Rico), on Albert Schweitzer. The colonizers are represented by Major Rice, a man who was raised in Africa and now fights to defend the colonizers' rights. Hansberry also introduces the character of the outside observer in the form of an American reporter who has come to write about the Mission.

Hansberry then takes us to a nearby hut where we meet three brothers, all African, but each touched by European influence. Tshembe is a world traveler now living in London with his European wife and son. Abioseh has never left his country, but has become a Catholic priest. Eric was born from the rape of his mother by a White man whose identity is concealed until near the climax of the play.

As mentioned above, Hansberry blends European tradition and African folklore to heighten the contrast between European and African culture and to highlight commonalities. When the radical Peter tells Tshembe a folklore about a laughing hyena, Tshembe replies, *"The Europeans have a similar tale which concerns a Danish prince."* A careful observer would have already noted connections between Tshembe and Hamlet. According to Carter, "both Hamlet and Hansberry's Tshembe Matoseh return from abroad for their father's funerals and both are confronted by spirits who demand that they act quickly to rid their countries of grave injustices." Like Shakespeare, Hansberry blends realism with non-realism creating a non-speaking female warrior character to visit Tshembe and remind him of his father's values. Both Tshembe and Hamlet take time to determine what they should do. In both plays, the guilty and the innocent die.

Hansberry allows the Black and White characters to make discoveries as tensions mount and violence fractures their world. Each must take a stand. Each is changed forever. *Les Blancs* is a deep, insightful work that merits our attention today. It is the work of a brilliant, gifted dramatist at the height of her powers. *Les Blancs* is an astonishing act of the imagination. Lorraine Hansberry never visited Africa, yet she marries all she studied and dreamed about Africa's landscape, culture, folklore and fight for freedom with her knowledge of European culture, stories and history of colonization to create a provocative drama. It is difficult to write a short essay on this profound play which can and has generated numerous studies and essays.

Hansberry began the play in 1960 just after *Raisin in the Sun* was produced. She had been thinking about and making notes on what would become the script, but reportedly was really spurred to write it after seeing the 1961 U.S. production of Jean Genet's *Les Negres* with James Earl Jones who would go on to play Tshembe, the main character in *Les Blancs*. According to Joy Abell (Lewis-Clark State College), Hansberry felt *Les Negres* was a conversation between white men about themselves. She was critical of Genet's assessment that Blacks would be as corrupt as Whites if they attained power. Abell reports she expressed to Robert Nemiroff (her ex-husband and producing partner) a desire to write a play "in which people of all ethnicities were equal participants in a much needed dialogue." *Les Blancs* is most certainly that play.

Unfortunately, Hansberry fell ill while writing the play. She managed, remarkably, to rehearse and open *The Sign in Sidney Brustein's Window* on Broadway and work on *Les Blancs* while undergoing treatment, literally carrying a typewriter and her notes in and out of hospitals. She wrote "If anything should happen-before 'tis done-may I trust that all commas and periods will be placed and someone will complete my thoughts . . . This last should be the least difficult since there are so many who think as I do."

After she passed away in 1965, Nemiroff, her literary executor, worked to keep her writing alive and to complete *Les Blancs* as he described it "along the lines we had explored together." He credits numerous people with helping him bring it to production in 1970, directed by John Berry with James Earl Jones and Earl Hyman among the actors. It was subsequently presented off-Broadway in 1980, at Arena Stage in 1988 and Huntington in 1989. The script **On Her Shoulders** is presenting was revised for a production at Oregon Shakespeare Festival in 1998. A 2003 production was done at the University of Wisconsin, with Lorraine Hansberry Visiting Professor Tim Bond directing. But it remains largely unproduced in the modern theatre.

The thing that makes you exceptional, if you are at all, is inevitably that which must also make you lonely.
—Lorraine Hansberry

Spunk
by Zora Neale Hurston

Directed by Aneesha Kudtarkar
Dramaturgy by Sadah "Espii" Proctor

Wednesday, April 15, 2015

Zora Neale Hurston: A Genius of the South
by Sadah "Espii" Proctor

Zora Neale Hurston was the "Queen of the Harlem Renaissance." A folklorist, anthropologist, and writer, Hurston integrated traditional African-American folklore into her writing. She lived during the Great Migration, when millions of African Americans moved from the South to the North for a better economic and social life. Unlike other Harlem Renaissance writers who focused on the African-American experience in the North, she centered many of her stories on life in the South. The subjects she covered led to conflicts and disagreements with her contemporaries resulting in a decline in her popularity.

Although she was born in Notasulga, Alabama in 1891, Zora Neale Hurston claimed in her autobiography, *Dust Tracks on the Road* (1942), that she was born in Eatonville, Florida in 1901. Hurston did not live in Eatonville until she was thirteen, when she moved there with her mother and father. Eatonville's status as the first incorporated all-black town in the country provided Hurston cultural inspiration for her stories surrounding black, rural life in the South. Hurston's upbringing in this self-governed town impacted her attitude about the boundaries in everyday rural African-American life, from self-determination to segregation to what was deemed "respectable" black art.

Hurston's parents were two former slaves: Lucy Ann Potts and John Hurston. Hurston's mother died in 1904. Her father, a pastor, remarried after her mother's death. Hurston spent the remainder of her childhood living with different family members and touring with a theatre troupe. She completed high school work at Morgan State University (then called Morgan Academy) in 1918, graduated from Howard University with an associate's degree in 1920, and entered Barnard College in New York to study anthropology in 1925. Hurston completed her bachelor's degree at Barnard and went on to graduate school at Columbia University.

Hurston experienced life in New York during the height of the Harlem Renaissance—a period of rebirth in African-American music, poetry, art and writing. She became acquainted with other figures like Langston Hughes, Countee Cullen, Wallace Thurman and Alain Locke, who dubbed the Harlem Renaissance the "New Negro Movement," a term indicating the new class and sophistication that African Americans were hoping to present in their lives and works at the turn of the century.

In 1926, Hurston joined with Hughes and Thurman to create *Fire!!*, a quarterly literary magazine reflecting the African-American experience during the Harlem Renaissance. Among many topics, it covered relationships, sexuality and intraracial prejudices. The magazine had poor sales and faced criticism that it did not fit with the "New Negro" image that African Americans wanted to portray in Harlem. Financial problems, coupled with the headquarters burning down, forced *Fire!!* to cease operations the same year, after publishing only one issue.

Hurston also began to clash with other writers of the Harlem Renaissance on the image of the "New Negro." Rather than adhere to the idealized image or focus on contentious issues facing the community, Hurston connected with African-American folklore and blues from the South in her work. In her most famous novel, *Their Eyes Were Watching God* (1937), she was criticized for trying too hard to appeal to whites, even though her immersion in folklore culture left a disconnect between her and white audiences. Her colleagues felt that she was utilizing minstrelsy images within language and dialect. In a letter she wrote to Countee Cullen in 1943, Hurston fired back at her critics, stating:

> "Just point out that we are suffering injustices and denied our rights, as if the white people did not know that already! Why don't I put something about lynchings in my books? As if all the world did not know about Negroes being

lynched! My stand is this: either we must do something about it that the white man will understand and respect, or shut up. No whiner ever got any respect or relief. If some of us must die for human justice, then let us die. For my own part, this poor body of mine is not so precious that I would not be willing to give it up for a good cause. But my own self-respect refuses to let me go to the mourner's bench."

Hurston studied various parts of the African diaspora in her anthropological research. Awarded a Guggenheim fellowship, she traveled to Jamaica and Haiti to study the folk religion Obeah. The Federal Writers Project also commissioned her to study African-American culture in Florida. Hurston had a fascination for conjure and voodoo culture that was prevalent in the South, particularly Louisiana and her hometown, Eatonville. She published her findings in works like *Mules and Men*, on African-American folklore; *Tell My Horse*, on her research about Obeah; *Seraph on the Swanee*, on the Diaspora experience in Honduras; and *Their Eyes Were Watching God*, which she wrote during her travels to Haiti.

Hurston faced financial problems toward the end of her life. She worked as a maid and journalist in Florida in the 1950s. Unfortunately, she suffered a stroke in 1959 and had to move into the St. Lucie County Welfare Home. On January 28, 1960, Zora Neale Hurston died of heart disease. She died alone, and because she had no money, was buried in an unmarked grave in her hometown of Eatonville, Florida. In 1973, writer Alice Walker rediscovered and brought attention back to Hurston's body of work. And in honor of the great writer and woman, Walker bought a headstone for Hurston's grave that read, "Zora Neale Hurston: A Genius of the South."

A Love Story, Plain and Simple
by Sadah "Espii" Proctor

When I went to school at Virginia Tech, I resided in a region called the New River Valley. It was a small segment of the Blue Ridge Mountains, which was part of an even larger range called the Appalachian Mountains. During my time there, I worked with local community members in a theatre project where people shared their stories about the region. We set time aside in the theatre to talk about their upbringing, their issues, their concerns and their ambitions. One of the ways we explored this was through music. I learned about how blues became bluegrass and eventually country music. I learned about how things were left behind as the music evolved. Instruments (the banjo, guitar), the "twang" and oral tradition became exaggerated stereotypes. Country music, distant from its ancestor, became a commodity to be bought and sold.

I think about how blues and jazz have this same relationship. While the blues emerged from African-American folk culture, jazz re-appropriated elements of the blues with "white" instruments: the piano, the trumpet, horns, etc. Blues focused on individual improvisation, while jazz had a set structure that a group could improvise within. Blues was mainly vocal, while jazz was instrumental. The heart of blues remained in the South and jazz became all the rage up North. Blues was something sung in the fields; jazz, on the other hand, had more commercial appeal.

During Zora Neale Hurston's time, the Great Migration was under way. Between 1910 and 1970, over six million African Americans moved from the South to the North. People moved to escape Jim Crow, to seek better economic opportunities with factory jobs and to exercise a new sense of freedom. Slavery was over. One of the significant things about the Harlem Renaissance was that its pioneers sought to create what they dubbed a "New Negro Movement"—the opportunity to reinvent the Negro as "sophisticated" and "educated." They sought to leave old things behind and embrace the new culture birthed in the North. Writers chronicled the struggles of the African-American condition in the North, the clashes that they faced with whites over jobs, segregation, justice and the lack of social and economic equality. African-American culture down South became "mammified" with the creation of minstrel shows. Accents were exaggerated, features were made fun of and even the blues tradition of singing and working were made into negative images that African-Americans up North wanted to abandon.

This divide is where Hurston was at odds with her colleagues of the Harlem Renaissance. A native Southerner, she grew up in an incorporated, all-black town. She came from a rich family and felt empowered by the black self-government around her. She didn't feel underprivileged or like a minority. While Hurston's contemporaries were reinventing the image of the Negro and exposing the discrimination he faced in the country, Hurston herself, never having felt slighted because of her race, opposed this approach. In her letter, *How It Feels To Be Colored Me*, she stated, "There is no great sorrow dammed up in my soul, nor lurking behind my eyes. I do not mind at all. I do not belong to the 40 sobbing school of Negrohood who hold that nature somehow has given them a low-down dirty deal and whose feelings are all hurt about it."

Spunk has all the elements that belong to a traditional love story. Boy meets girl, and they fall in love; someone/something threatens to tear them apart; and despite the odds, they come together in the end. The remarkable thing about *Spunk* is that it is a love story sprinkled with aspects of southern, African-American culture. There is talk about conjuring and hoodoo, new beginnings and the church, the nonchalant attitudes of whites towards African Americans when there is "order," blues music and the rich use of dialect by all of the characters. There is no idealistic picture of life in SPUNK nor any lamentation on any existing conditions. Everything exists as it is. Hurston forged her own path during the Harlem Renaissance by holding onto what she loved and grew up with in Eatonville. What was seen as "the old ways" by many African Americans during the Great Migration was brought to light in her work, and rather than looking down the road to the future, Hurston's work held a mirror up to African-American culture in her present time. This approach of immersing her audience into her world made her a noted figure, but it cost her popularity.

Today, we honor Zora Neale Hurston for shedding light on different components of the African diaspora, remaining true to her own vision of the world in which she lived and for being bold enough to express it publicly.

No matter how far a person can go, the horizon is still way beyond you.
—Zora Neale Hurston

"Soul Struggle"
Blue Blood, Plumes, Blue-Eyed Black Boy, Starting Point
by Georgia Douglas Johnson

Directed by **Elizabeth Van Dyke**
Dramaturgy by **Arminda Thomas**

Wednesday, February 17, 2016

So Much Lost, But Not Forgotten by Melissa Attebery

We know that Georgia Blanche Douglas Camp Johnson was born on September 10th in Atlanta, GA, to parents of African American, Native American, and English descent, but the actual year of her birth, some time between the years of 1877 and 1887, has been lost to history. She may have intentionally concealed her age, but the loss of this detail is more reflective of the difficulties she faced as a woman, an African American and an artist in a time when expectations directly conflicted with but could not suppress her calling. In spite of her obstacles, she became the best known and most widely published African American woman poet of the Harlem Renaissance, as well as an accomplished playwright and journalist.

She graduated from the Normal School of Atlanta University some time between 1893 and 1896, and for about ten years, taught school in Atlanta and Marietta. She was a self-taught violinist and church organist, so she went on to formally study music at the Oberlin Conservatory of Music and the Cleveland College of Music (and possibly at Howard University in Washington, D.C., although this detail is also lost to history).

She fell in love with Henry Lincoln Johnson, a prominent attorney and Republican politician, who expected her to become a housewife and to take primary responsibility for raising their children, so she resigned her position as an Atlanta school principal to marry him in 1903. Encouraged by poet William Stanley Braithwaite, she published her first poem in 1905 in an anthology called *Voice of the Negro* and began to take herself seriously as a poet. She gave birth to two sons between 1906 and 1907, then in 1909 or 1910, looking to establish his own law firm, her husband moved them all to Washington, D.C., where he was later appointed by President Taft to the prestigious position of Recorder of Deeds for the District of Columbia.

Her busy life as a politician's wife and mother didn't leave a lot of time for writing, but it did broaden her view of the world, as she came into contact with the Black elite society of Washington, D.C., including writer Jean Toomer. Determined to express her art, in 1916, at about 36 years old, she managed to get three of her poems published in *The Crisis*, the official magazine of the NAACP.

She published her first volume of poetry, *The Heart of a* Woman, in 1918, expressing the sorrowful voice of an artist whose talents never fully developed due to the conventions of her time. Her second volume, *Bronze* (1922), clarified this internalization of a diminished existence, thus establishing her as an important female African American poet.

In the early 1920s, Toomer encouraged Johnson to host a weekly open house at her now historic home at 1461 S Street NW, in Washington, D.C. These meetings of the "Saturday Nighters" allowed her to showcase her gracious hospitality, which pleased her husband, but more importantly, enhanced her standing among the notable African American writers of the time. The "S Street Salon," as it came to be known, was a "safe and supportive" atmosphere "where Harlem Renaissance writers struggled with their literary work and where that work found its first audience." Johnson called it her "Half-Way House," because she was always willing to shelter artists in need, including, at one point, Zora Neale Hurston. The S Street Salon became one of the greatest literary salons of the Harlem Renaissance, and was attended by Langston Hughes, Angelina Weld Grimké, Braithwaite, W.E.B. DuBois, Alice Dunbar-Nelson, Jessie Redmon Fauset and Alain Locke.

When her husband died in 1925, Johnson's popularity as a writer was at its peak. But now, at 45 years old, in order to support her two sons, she had to work temp jobs as a substitute public school teacher and a file clerk for the Civil Service. She did some hack writing, using a variety of pen names, which unfortunately rendered much of her work lost to future generations. She finally found stable work with the Commissioner of

Immigration for the Department of Labor, where the hours were long and the pay low, but she still managed to help put her sons through college, then through law school and medical school, while still continuing to host the Saturday Nighters.

In 1926, she began to write plays with female central characters. Most of the plays were lost (thrown away after her death by family members who did not understand their importance), and few were recovered, but according to her "Catalogue of Writings," which she put together in 1962/63, she wrote 28 plays. Plays such as *Plumes*, which won first prize for a drama on Black life (in a contest run by the academic journal *Opportunity: A Journal of Negro Life* in 1927) helped to drive the community-based New Negro Little Theatre movement of the era.

Johnson was also a key advocate in the anti-lynching movement and so was a pioneering member of the lynching drama tradition. Six of her plays, including *A Sunday Morning in the South* and *Blue-Eyed Black Boy*, were written as activist pieces in the campaign against lynching, although none were published or produced during her lifetime. Although she was involved in the NAACP's anti-lynching campaigns of 1936 and 1938, the NAACP refused to produce many of her plays, claiming they gave a feeling of hopelessness, which was her intention as she did not feel hopefulness was a realistic outcome.

Her third volume of poetry, *An Autumn Love Cycle* (1928), is considered to be her best book of poetry and focuses on love later in life.

Johnson traveled extensively in the late 1920s, giving lectures and readings, wrote a weekly newspaper column, "Homely Philosophy," that was syndicated by twenty publications between 1926 and 1932, and organized and ran an international correspondence club from 1930 to 1965. Her "Catalogue of Writings" also noted over 200 poems, 31 short stories, a book-length manuscript about her literary salon, a novel and a biography of her late husband. Of the 31 short stories, only three have been located, under the pseudonym of Paul Tremaine. It's possible that this missing material was also thrown away after her death.

Her catalogue notes that she also wrote many songs and produced at least two dozen "written and copyrighted" songs, including a "Georgia State College School Song" (for what would become Savannah State University). She even collaborated with the classical singer and composer Lillian Evanti on several published pieces in the late 1940s. Johnson self-published her final book of poetry, *Share My World*, in 1962. Influenced by the wisdom gained from her lifetime, its poems deal with the oneness of humankind and contain generous forgiveness and a love towards all.

In 1965, in recognition of her meaningful achievements and their reflection upon "her native city, her alma mater, her race, and humanity," Atlanta University presented Johnson with an honorary doctorate of literature. She died shortly thereafter in 1966 in Washington, D.C. In September 2009, Johnson was inducted into the Georgia Writers Hall of Fame.

Georgia Douglas Johnson: From Poet to Playwright
by Arminda Thomas

By the time Georgia Douglas Johnson turned her hand to playwriting, she was already recognized as a major poetic voice in the New Negro movement (which would in time be called the Harlem Renaissance). She had published two books of poetry, *The Heart of a Woman* (1918) and *Bronze* (1922), and her poems regularly appeared in the NAACP's *Crisis* and the National Urban League's *Opportunity* magazines. In addition, her weekly informal gatherings of artists, intellectuals and activists were fast making her Washington D.C. home ("The Half-Way House," she called it) a destination spot in African-American civic and cultural life—a place where Langston Hughes and Wallace Thurman could dream up a literary magazine for more experimental writing, where A. Philip Randolph could make his case for unionizing sleeping-car porters to the city's disapproving black elite, and where Carter G. Woodson (educator and organizer of Negro History Week) could convince playwrights May Miller and Willis Richardson to curate an anthology "dramatizing every phase of [Negro] life and history" as a learning tool for African-American schoolchildren. That book, *Negro History in Thirteen Plays*, included two of Johnson's works.

Johnson's entry into playwriting was encouraged by various friends, including Zona Gale (the first woman to be awarded the Pulitzer Prize in drama), Alain Locke, curator and herald of the New Negro movement, and NAACP co-founder W.E.B. Du Bois. The rise of the Little Theatre movement, along with the trend towards serious dramas, focused on the lives of common people—including "Negroes"—had created an opportunity for the birth of an authentic African American drama, which Locke, Du Bois and others in the community were eager to encourage (though they often differed on the form that drama should take). To that end, *Opportunity* and *Crisis* magazines began offering playwriting contests with cash prizes; and in order to provide a venue (and, it was hoped, to build an audience) for the works, small theatre groups sprouted up in African American communities, schools, and organizations across the country.

The short lifespan (and dearth of record-keeping) for many of these venues, along with the destruction of most of Johnson's own papers after her death, makes it difficult to say with certainty how many of Johnson's plays received productions in her lifetime. It seems clear, however, that two of her earliest plays were her most "successful" in terms of publications and acclamation.

Blue Bloods, a one-act comedy that manages to tackle the absurdity of colorism in the context of sexual exploitation, was awarded honorable mention in *Opportunity*'s 1926 contest. It was published as a single play by Appleton-Century and subsequently anthologized in Alain Locke and Montgomery Gregory's *Plays of Negro Life* (1927) and in Frank Shay's *50 More Contemporary One-Act Plays* (1938). *Blue Blood* was staged by Du Bois' Krigwa Players in New York in 1927 and by the Howard University Players in 1933.

Johnson's next play, *Plumes*, was also well received. After taking first place in *Opportunity*'s contest, *Plumes* was published by Samuel French in 1927 and later appeared in Locke and Gregory's anthology, as well as V.F. Calverton's *Anthology of American Negro Literature*. Set in the rural south, *Plumes* brings us an impoverished woman struggling to choose whether to spend her life's savings on a surgery that might possibly save her beloved daughter's life—or to save the money for the daughter's funeral. It was produced by the Harlem Experimental Theatre (1927) and Chicago's Cube Theater (1928). Aside from the two pieces included in Richardson and Miller's historical drama anthology, *Plumes* and *Blue Blood* were the only plays to be published in Johnson's lifetime.

As the 1920s gave way to the bleaker '30s, the Harlem Renaissance began to lose steam. *Crisis* and *Opportunity* turned their focus away from the arts. The Krigwa Players and Harlem Experimental Theatre disbanded. The opportunities for playwrights to see their work staged were dwindling. Langston Hughes recalled:

> We were no longer in vogue, anyway, we Negroes. Sophisticated New Yorkers turned to Noel Coward. Colored actors began to go hungry, publishers politely rejected new manuscripts, and patrons found other uses for their money.

Some relief came in the form of the Federal Theatre Project, which was created to ease the high levels of unemployment in the arts communities. The FTP even established Negro Troupes in several cities. The plays Johnson submitted to the FTP met with mixed reviews, and ultimately none were selected for production. Her plays about lynching met with particular criticism: some objected to the static nature of the pieces, as Johnson's plays were all set away from the murderous crowds in an effort to hone in on the effect the barbaric practice had on the victims' family, friends and neighbors. Another remarked disapprovingly that Johnson trivialized the offences that led to lynching, when "in *fact* the crime that produces lynching is far fouler."

The lynching plays also met resistance where she might have expected none. When Johnson sent her lynching plays to NAACP Executive Secretary Walter White for possible production by the Youth Council, he replied that the Council had rejected the pieces because "they all ended in defeat." Johnson replied, "It is true that in life things don't end usually ideally." In this more recent era of unwarranted police shootings caught on video, of the Black Lives Matter movement, some theatre groups have revisited Johnson's lynching plays. Theater for a New City included one, *The Blue-Eyed Black Boy*, in a 2015 production of "lost" one-acts from the Harlem Renaissance. Of the six lynching plays that Johnson penned, this play comes closest to White's desired triumphant ending. The mother is able, in the end, to convince someone to save her son—though the reason she succeeds is not ideal.

In one of her later plays, *The Starting Point* (1938), Johnson captures the heartbreak and disappointment of an elderly couple who have invested all their hopes and treasure on a beloved son, only to have him squander it all. In order to save him, they must convince him to accept a life of radically diminished expectations. It is a work that may well reflect the disappointment that Johnson and others of her generation experienced as the post-Renaissance years left most of them scrambling for opportunities that had once seemed certain. Still, there is resilience in the old couple, as there was in their creator, who continued to write—and to nurture and champion other writers—for the rest of her life.

The world is as big as you make it.
—Georgia Douglas Johnson

A Fool of Fortune
by Martha Morton

Directed by **Melody Brooks**
Dramaturgy by **Sherry Engle**

Wednesday, February 19, 2014

Dean of the Women Playwrights **by Sherry Engle**

Martha Morton was born in NYC on October 10, 1865, the sixth of eight children to Amelia and Joseph Morton, a china importer. Morton credited her mother, "an ardent student of Shakespeare," for transmitting to her a taste for reading plays. But playwriting was apparently in her genes, since literary ancestors included Thomas Morton (c. 1764-1838), a well-known English dramatist and his son, John Maddison Morton (1811-1891), who wrote comedies, melodramas, and farces. When she was ten, the Morton family returned to London, residing in Regent's Park where the Morton children were exposed to literary and theatrical figures. Morton maintained in interviews that her earliest writing as a child consisted of poems and short stories; when her mother suggested she send a story to a magazine, it was accepted, earning the budding writer twenty-five dollars. In the early 1880s, she attended the Normal College (Hunter), although health problems apparently kept her from graduating.

Morton wrote a number of early plays, but secured her first public showing with a parody of David Belasco's popular musical, *May Blossom,* a piece she had written to amuse friends. When producer Daniel Frohman heard of the skit, he used it in a benefit in May 1885. After failed attempts to interest theatre managers in her full-length, *Hélène,* Morton rented the Fifth Avenue Theatre on a Monday night for a preview to a packed house. Set in France, the play reflects typical melodramas of the day, revolving around a misunderstood heroine and the two men who love her. In spite of unflattering reviews, the play attracted the attention of Clara Morris, known for her highly emotive acting style in playing tragic heroines. Morris' production of *Hélène* ran for a week in October of 1889 at the Union Square Theatre and became the chief feature of her touring season, netting the playwright $50,000. Riding on the play's commercial success, Morton wrote a novelized version, published as *Hélène Buderoff; or, A Strange Duel* in 1889. Thus, at the age of twenty Martha Morton began what would become a 30-year playwriting career—an accomplishment which had not until then been achieved by any American woman.

Subsequent plays set in America show that Morton took her cousin Edward Arthur's advice to "throw away that French trash. Look at the life about you and write of that." She claimed she grew up knowing the "ups and downs" of the merchant life, most likely through her father and brothers' experiences. *The Merchant* (1890) focuses on a desperate business man on the brink of financial ruin and the crisis it causes on his marriage. The "new-school" trend was utilized in Morton's third play, *Geoffrey Middleton, Gentleman*, through contemporary scenes considered "quiet and natural." The play tells of aristocratic Geoffrey Middleton who marries for money, not for himself, but for his father. When husband and wife actually fall in love, they must first clear up assumptions about one another and their marriage.

Early on, Morton garnered attention as a playwright, in part because she was succeeding in a man's profession. An interview in the *Dramatic Mirror* (11-7-1891) states "Miss Morton is the latest recruit to the ranks of our native playwrights. The fact that she is a woman imparts an added interest to the event." Her work ethic was often noted: her daily writing schedule, dedication to learning the craft, attending every performance and closely monitoring the audience, as well as directing her own plays. In addition, 1890s articles continued to tout her "pecuniary" success and the income generated through runs of plays—which very likely drew more women to the profession. When asked why there were not more women who were successful as dramatists, Morton stated it was because most of those who attempted to write plays were "appalled" by the difficulties encountered. What was more, it was not so easy for a woman to acquire the practical knowledge of theatre as it was for a man.

After her father died in August 1895, it fell to Martha to provide primary support for her mother and her un-married sisters. At the age of thirty-two, on 25 August 1897, she married Hermann Conheim, an established New York business man who had immigrated to the U.S. from Germany at age eighteen. The Conheims lived at 265 West 90th Street, their home described as handsome and even "rarely beautiful." While they never had children, their twenty-eight year marriage remained mutually supportive.

Morton returned from her honeymoon in time for the opening of *A Bachelor's Romance* with comedian Sol Smith Russell, which ultimately proved to be her most popular play throughout the U.S. and Great Britain. Audiences enjoyed the wholesome humor and various subplots in a play that has four romantic pairings at the end. Although Morton followed up with at least ten more plays, none would achieve the commercial and public success of *A Bachelor's Romance*—it was made into a film in 1915. Morton continued fulfilling orders for managers and star actors, but her writing began to express attitudes about women not always received favor-ably by critics or audiences. *Her Lord and Master*, a 1902 play about a spunky American woman who meets and marries a wealthy British man, proved to be a comedy of manners with a bite, an exposé of American attitudes and culture. Perhaps most damning of American women was her 1907 drama, *The Movers*, in which the excessive spending and reckless Wall Street investing by a young couple leads to the husband's suicide; Marion, his wife, must then examine her feverish pursuit of material gain and reform her ways. Morton then created the heroic Anna, a highborn young woman who sacrifices herself in the Russian revolution in a 1909 adaptation of Leopold Kampf's *On the Eve*. In her last professional New York production, *Three of Hearts*, Morton tried her hand at the detective play, which had come into vogue around 1903.

Most of Martha Morton's work, like many plays written during the Progressive Era, is now unknown to modern audiences and barely receives mention in theatre history texts. Even so, her leadership among women dramatists in the formation of the Society of Dramatic Authors in January 1909 when the American Dramatists' Club refused admission to women remains one of her most significant contributions to American theatre. By the time she died at the age of sixty on February 19, 1925, her *New York Times* obituary cited Morton as "one of the first women to write plays successfully in America." In the latter part of her notable career, she served as mentor and role model for young aspiring women dramatists.

Star Struck! by Sherry Engle

Once she began achieving success with early productions, Martha Morton received requests from managers and actors to adapt works or create star vehicles. The star who undoubtedly boosted Morton's career into greater prominence was actor-comedian William H. Crane. When Morton's *Brother John* opened with Crane in 1893, he had been acting for close to thirty years and his appearances in New York were always highly anticipated by fans who enjoyed his broad humor. Morton created for him the character of John Hackett, a prosperous hatter with a factory in rural Connecticut, who provides for and dominates the lives of his younger siblings. Her second play for the actor provided an equally suitable role. In *His Wife's Father*, which she condensed and adapted from a four-act German farce, Crane plays Buchanan Billings, a wealthy grocer and doting father, who becomes a meddlesome father when his only child marries.

In spite of the monetary rewards of tailoring plays for Crane, after *His Wife's Father* Morton suggested to the comedian that the public needed to see him in "something not by Martha Morton," that after a break, she "would write for him again if he wished it." One wonders if perhaps writing for a prominent comedian (who most likely changed or added lines during performances) had its drawbacks. Had Morton, as the "subservient" playwright, begun to feel overshadowed by the star performer? The lack of discernment on the part of Crane's fans certainly reflects the difficulty for a playwright who wished to be taken seriously by critics and audiences. Possibly Morton felt a need to develop more complex characters and themes, or she simply decided it would be a wise "marketing" strategy to temporarily break away from Crane, as she put it, "for the benefit of the public, Mr. Crane, and myself." Although the comedian agreed, he came to see her several months later, urging her to write another play for him and suggested a Wall Street theme. A few days later Morton proposed an idea for a storyline of a play and with Crane's approval, she began creating "a part entirely different from anything he had done before," and a year later she read the first draft of the play to the actor.

The role was that of Elisha Cuningham, a successful investor at the point of retiring in luxury who returns from Europe only to discover his partner has "involved him in a speculation which, through the treachery of a financial associate, reduces him to penury." Cuningham takes to drink and becomes a wreck, but with the help of his daughter's suitor, he effectively turns the tables on the man who ruined him. The victory is bittersweet though and the ending was completely unexpected. Morton describes Crane's horrified reaction:

> "When we came to the death scene, he exclaimed in a startled way: '*Why, Martha! I can't die. Dear me, no! You'll have to fix it some other way.*' But I persuaded him that was the only logical and legitimate ending which the story could have; that without it the play would be absolutely unconvincing."

Although discussion continued over the ending (including experimenting with another ending in tryouts), *A Fool of Fortune* opened as written on December 1, 1896 to favorable critical reception. The *New York Times* compared *A Fool of Fortune*'s "stock ticker" theme to *The Henrietta*, calling it "the best of its kind since that comedy by Bronson Howard, which is the best American play ever written. *A Fool of Fortune* represents one of Morton's more enduring works; when Crane and Company revived the play in 1912 in a special matinee performance, the *New York Times* declared the story to be "quite as fresh today as it was in 1896."

Fifteen years after *A Fool of Fortune* debuted, Morton created a light-hearted comedic role for William H. Crane in *The Senator Keeps House,* not only marking her reunion with the actor, but also his fiftieth season on the American stage. At this time the hearty production at the Garrick Theatre, opening November 1911 and running for 80 performances must have provided a boost for Morton, as it had been about nine years since she had enjoyed a healthy run.

Interesting to note is that in the original script of *A Fool of Fortune*, Powers, the "Big Operator," is described as a "quick, ratty kind of man, like Russell Sage, shabby, tall, gaunt and thin." The playwright creates a nervous character, fast-talking and heartless, yet in spite of his treachery delivers some comical lines. The "model" for this character, Russell Sage, was a financier, railroad executive and Whig politician who was frequently a partner of Jay Gould, a notorious stock trader. Sage amassed a vast fortune. Although Morton's impression of Sage seems to be that of a "villain," after his death his widow distributed most of his wealth to educational institutions and established Russell Sage College in Troy, New York.

---

1. *New York Times*, 2 December 1896, 5.
2. Crane in *A Fool of Fortune*," *New York Times*, 13 January 1912, 7.
3. *Boston Evening Traveler*, 9 August 1898, n.p.
4. Ibid.

It was fore-ordained by heredity that I should write.
—Martha Morton

Madame La Mort and Pleasure
by Rachilde

Directed by **Melissa Attebery**
Dramaturgy by **Melody Brooks**

Wednesday, July 16, 2014

Rachilde: Not a Symbol **by Melody Brooks**

Paris theatre in the 1890s was mostly closed to women playwrights—but as she did with so many other areas of her life, Rachilde shattered that barrier and played a major role in the formation of the Symbolist Theatre. Her writing and behind-the-scenes involvement ensured the creation of the first art theatres in Europe, the Théâtre d'Art and the Théâtre de l'Oeuvre, and she is even credited with having coined the term "absurd" for the new style of non-realistic drama. In her day she hosted a salon that attracted the most prominent members of the French symbolist movement as well as international celebrities such as Oscar Wilde, Rudyard Kipling, H.G. Wells and Friedrich Nietzsche.

Born Marguerite Eymery on February 11, 1860, her multiple memoirs give conflicting stories of her youth—some claim a hateful mother, others a drunken father, still others of having been raised as a boy. Her education was informal, but due to parental neglect she had free use of her publisher grandfather's library—a largely unsuitable collection for a young woman at the time, with works by the Marquis de Sade purportedly among her selections. She was writing from at least the age of 12, with short stories published in a local paper, preoccupied with sexual identity and gender norms. She took the name "Rachilde" at 17, supposedly that of a Swedish nobleman who appeared to her in a séance, after a note of encouragement from her idol Victor Hugo convinced her that she was destined to become a professional writer. Her new name became not only a pseudonym but a new identity—carefully crafted and rigorously maintained throughout her lifetime.

She moved to Paris at the age of 21 and begin writing articles on ladies' fashion to support herself. She joined avant-garde literary circles—including those identifying as Symbolists. In 1884, her novel *Mr. Venus*, with a cross-dressing female protagonist, was published in Belgium and became a *succès de scandale* when Rachilde was sentenced to prison in absentia. The French edition included a preface that titillated the general public with the revelation that the novel had been written by an innocent, unmarried young woman. Rachilde gained immediate notoriety and her Tuesday salon became the place for young literary people to meet. Symbolist poets called her the "queen of the decadents." Although she maintained an aura of personal innocence, respectable hostesses refused to receive her, and she continued to write best-selling novels—many of which addressed sexuality, gender reversals and death.

She also continued to construct and develop her image. Rachilde cut her hair short and dyed it blond at the age of 25, and more outrageously for the time, applied to the police for permission to wear men's clothes in public—claiming that as a journalist who traveled alone to questionable areas she would feel safer. Her request was denied but drawings and one photograph survive of Rachilde dressed as a man. It's unclear whether this was a regular occurrence, but cross-dressing became part of her myth. Her calling card read "Rachilde, Man of Letters" and fellow Symbolists addressed her as "brother writer"—even though many also wrote love sonnets to her green eyes and "unconquerable virginity." She was wearing a man's suit at a ball in 1885 when she met Alfred Vallette, whom she married four years later. Her new calling card read "Rachilde, Madame Alfred Vallette" and her only child, Gabrielle, was born in 1890 (or late 1889.)

She did not, however, settle into domesticity. Instead she put her energy into *Mercure de France*, the literary journal her husband helped create in tandem with the birth of her daughter. She now held her salon at the newspaper—which became the premier avant-garde journal in Paris. One of the goals of the *Mercure* was to foster a Symbolist Theatre—a "theatre of the soul"—where the physical world would be less important than a mystical inner life. She wrote her first two plays for the Théâtre d'Art, with *Voice of Blood* premiering November 18, 1890.

An influential reviewer, Ernest Raynaud wrote, "It is a play with cruel observation and studied construction, in spite of its apparent simplicity...This play is written in a virile way. It teems with wit, which will surprise no one, coming from Rachilde, a writer whose sharp, caustic talent people do not prize enough—however highly they may esteem it. It is true that Rachilde is a woman and we are molded with prejudices with regard to women...The characters are developed with skill and show that the author has scenic aptitudes of the first order." Eugene Cros called the play "theatre without flim-flam or artifice, real at last!" Rachilde joined the committee that chose plays for the Théâtre d'Art and Paul Fort, its founder, began a close association with the writers at *Mercure*. Her second play, *Madame La Mort*, was performed in March 1891, again to critical acclaim.

In addition to her plays, Rachilde was a prolific author in other media: she published nineteen books between 1884 and 1900, and critiqued novels for a column for the *Mercure*, often reading and commenting on as many as forty books a month. Then her momentum slowed. Between 1901 and 1912 she published only four books. After World War I, her writing took on a darker, more cynical nature; some conjecture that she may in fact have been a manic-depressive. *The Painted Woman*, published in 1921, deals most explicitly with violence in sexual relations. Apparently never performed in her lifetime, it was her only play to deal directly with the war and anticipates ideas that she explored further in *Le Grand Seigneur* (literally, *The Grand Bloodletter*, with a pun on the word seignor, or lord) published in 1922.

By this time, however, Rachilde and her husband were out of step with the times. They ridiculed the Dadaist movement and she lost potential support from the feminists when she published a pamphlet in 1928, "Why I Am Not a Feminist." She was still known for crazy escapades and surprising energy but after her husband died suddenly in 1935, she stopped receiving visitors at her salon. Her eyesight was failing and she had difficulty walking, but she needed to write to survive, and so she did. Rachilde published her last novel in 1942 and continued to live above the *Mercure de France* offices in an apartment without a telephone. Her daughter was the only regular visitor, and by the time she died on April 4, 1953 at the age of 93, Rachilde was virtually forgotten as a writer.

A Theatre of the Soul **by Melody Brooks**

The Symbolist Movement began in the late 19th century in France with the publication of *Les Fleurs du mal* (*The Flowers of Evil*, 1857) by **Charles Baudelaire**. It was a reaction against the trend toward naturalism and realism; the works of **Edgar Allan Poe** were the source of many stock tropes and images for symbolists. They were interested in the connections between the visible and invisible and believed the deeper truths of existence (known intuitively) could not be directly expressed but only indirectly revealed by endowing particular images or objects with symbolic meaning.

The term was first used by the critic **Jean Moréas** who published his *Symbolist Manifesto* in *Le Figaro* on September 18, 1886. Mysticism and otherworldliness, mortality and the power of sexuality were characteristic of the style. One of the most successful journals dedicated to Symbolism was *Le Mercure de France*, edited by Alfred Vallette, Rachilde's husband. Founded in 1890 (almost coincidental with their marriage and birth of their daughter), the pair turned the *Mercure* into the guiding light of the movement. They were the power-couple of their time, mentoring and supporting the vanguard of the avant-garde, including such luminaries of the demi-monde as Colette and Alfred Jarry.

Rachilde made a more direct contribution to the success of a Symbolist Theatre through her own plays—she wrote 20 of them which were performed across Europe and in Russia. *Madame la Mort* and *Volupté* are two significant achievements in the development and realization of a true Symbolist aesthetic. *Madame la Mort* is only Rachilde's second play but it advanced the ideal of transcending the limitations of a physical stage and human actors. Produced at **Théâtre d'Art** in 1891, extensive program notes explain her intention: "The first scenes of the drama unfold *somewhere in life*; but the second act takes place entirely in a dream, *inside the mind of a dying man*, and since these death throes are caused by a powerful poison...I tried to render palpable certain hallucinations, namely: the battle between Life and Death, who fight for the soul of the neurotic man, each using their best arguments."

The play was a critical success—it meshed with the value symbolists placed on the inner versus the physical life. Although Acts I and III appeared realistic, Rachilde offered further program notes, which seem to have aided appreciation of the play. She wrote, "In saying: *cerebral drama*, I wanted to indicate that it concerns an action *which, strictly speaking,* has no locale...And if there is a setting called the *smoking room*, or the *living room*, another called the *garden*, that is because it would be very difficult for everything to happen completely in the clouds. So I beg the spectators to let the setting count for almost nothing."

Given that prior productions at the Théâtre d'Art had been derided for the poor quality and skimpiness of the sets, perhaps she felt it necessary to excuse a lack of resources to fully achieve her vision; perhaps it was meant to free audiences' imaginations from any obligation to the visual. Regardless, several of the critics did find hidden or allegorical meanings throughout the play.

But it was the second act that received the most attention. Reviewers described it as "the stuff of dreams"; "of remarkable dramatic movement and conciseness...a real coup, the loftiest thing the author has ever written"; "like a poem by Edgar Poe...the strange work of an artist"; "something original, curious, new, never seen before, refreshing..." None of them described the physical setting for Act II in any detail however. Rachilde had commissioned a drawing by Paul Gauguin of "The Veiled Woman" for the playbill. Her thinness now looks chic, but in 1891 it was not an attractive quality (and indeed the actress Georgette Camée had previously been deemed too skinny by some critics). Alfred Vallette wrote that "Death is maternal" in his review, and yet the Veiled Woman is the voice of power in the play. In Rachilde's notes to the actors in the original manuscript, she explains that the characters in the garden are more like forms in a dream than living creatures and that the actors needed to speak with a less resonant voice than usual.

Apparently only Cameé was successful at this, and in the subsequent published version the playwright made several changes to Act II, especially in the punctuation and stage directions. Notably many sentences now ended with ellipses instead of periods or exclamation marks, suggesting lengthy pauses (for the symbolists, the supernatural entered in the long silences and they became a hallmark of absurdist drama). She delineated movement patterns for *The Veiled Woman,* and inserted character descriptions—possibly influenced by Cameé's performance but certainly to limit the degree to which actors might misinterpret her intentions as the original "Paul" had done. Remembering the production more than 30 years later, when asked why she no longer wrote for theatre, Rachilde said, "Because I don't like it. Those rehearsals where you see everything you have pictured torn to shreds....you can't fulfill what the mind has imagined, in the theatre...so what good is it?"

Pleasure (Volupté) appeared in *Mercure* in 1893 but it was not performed until 1896. This play fully achieved the slow-moving, almost somnambulistic atmosphere that Symbolist Theatre had been trying to create, but it is also the most overtly sexual of Rachilde's dramas. Prior to the production she wrote to a friend that the performance would be far better than the published version, as Paul Franck, who played the boy had "completely revised" the play. "It was stupid before he fixed it...you'll see." No copy of the revised script exists, but in this premiere performance, the two young lovers played at strangling each other and the boy ended up killing the girl. Critics supportive of the symbolist aesthetic praised the play, but mainstream reviewers found it morbid and incomprehensible. The published version (with the original ending) gives more power to the girl (perhaps this is why Franck felt the need for a change in that first performance?) Camille Mauclair (novelist and *fin de siècle* chronicler) said that Rachilde had "invented a modern fear" without affectation or pomposity, in one of the "most interesting plays of the season." The ambiguous ending certainly anticipates the Theatre of the Absurd.

Indeed, Rachilde's plays and her life's work in general paved the way for Artaud, Grotowski, Ionesco, Genet, Beckett, Pinter, Albee, Stoppard, and an avant-garde yet to come. Ironically, her sexual politics and sardonic humor make her work more performable today than many of her more famous male contemporaries.

> *For the greatest happiness of women is to be right one day, one hour, one second after being wrong all their lives . . . apparently.*
> —Rachilde

The Group
by Mercy Otis Warren

Directed by **Kristin Heckler**
Dramaturgy by **Melody Brooks**

April 13, 2016

Mercy Otis Warren: No "Adulator" by Melody Brooks

Mercy Otis Warren was a poet, dramatist, satirist, patriot propagandist, and historian who was one of the first U.S. women to write specifically for publication (even when her work was anonymous.). She was the third child of James Otis and Mary Allyne, of Barnstable, south of Plymouth, on Cape Cod. Otis was a farmer, merchant, and attorney, and was elected to the Massachusetts House of Representatives in 1745. Not having an education himself, he wanted his two sons to attend college and hired his brother-in-law the Reverend Jonathan Russell to tutor them. When Joseph, the oldest, declined the education, Mercy was allowed to take his place. She studied the same curriculum as her brother James, except for Latin and Greek, which she read in translation. She also appears to have shared in his studies for his Masters Degree. They were exceptional students and both became excellent writers and rhetoricians. It was the younger James who first uttered the phrase "Taxation without representation is tyranny," which became the battle cry for the American Revolution. Mercy's writing is filled with historical references and characters in classical literature, her two favorite subjects of study.

In 1754, Mercy married James Warren, a farmer from Plymouth and a Harvard classmate of her brother. They had a long, happy marriage and raised five sons. Like the Otis men, Warren was elected to the Massachusetts House of Representatives. He served from 1766 to 1778, eventually becoming Speaker and then president of the Massachusetts Provincial Congress. A radical and outspoken activist, he was a leader in local revolutionary politics, and his wife was a worthy partner in his endeavors.

No other woman, with the possible exception of Abigail Adams, was as intimately involved with the politics of the day. Warren was continually at or near the center of events for more than two decades, from the Stamp Act crisis of 1765 to the establishment of the federal republic in 1789. Her Plymouth home was the gathering place of patriot leaders for ten years preceding the Revolution. These meetings laid the foundation for the Committees of Correspondence, the first organized efforts to form a unified resistance across the thirteen colonies to the so-called "Intolerable Acts" of the British Parliament.

The first Committees were temporary, such as that opposing the Stamp Act, and they were disbanded when the objective was achieved. But as the situation moved from resistance to revolution, permanent committees were established to inform the voters of the common threat faced by all the colonies, and to disseminate information from the cities to the rural communities where most of the people lived. The news was spread through letters and printed pamphlets, and promulgated the patriots' view and version of events. In answer to a query by Mercy early on as to the appropriateness of a woman stepping into the propagandist fray, her ardent fan and cheerleader, John Adams, wrote to her husband:

> "Tell your wife that God Almighty (I use a bold style) has entrusted her with Powers for the good of the World, which, in the Cause of His Providence, he bestows on few of the human race. That instead of being a fault to use them, it would be criminal to neglect them."

Warren did indeed use her "Powers" for the revolutionary cause. She wrote numerous letters and poems, which she published anonymously in newspapers and pamphlets. Her most effective efforts at propaganda were a series of satirical plays—considered the first written by a U.S. woman. They appeared serially in news-papers and as pamphlets, but were not performed, because Puritan Boston had laws against staging plays and did not have a theater until 1794.

In 1781 as the fighting ended, the Warrens were given the estate of their former nemesis, Governor Thomas Hutchinson (the "Rapatio" of *The Group)*, but lived there only eight years before moving back to Plymouth, where Mercy continued writing. In 1790, she became the third American woman following Anne Bradstreet and Phyllis Wheatley to publish a significant collection of poetry in her own name. *Poems, Dramatic and Mis-*

cellaneous included poems written before and during the war. It began with a humble dedication to George Washington and contained two more plays, *The Sack of Rome* and *The Ladies of Castille*.

Both works dramatize historical analogues to the American Revolution and explore another important theme in Warren's satires and poetry: the issue of women as writers and revolutionary activists. And although the question of Warren's "feminism" has been a subject of much debate, these plays do cast women and mothers as public orators and rebel leaders, and give them the most stirring speeches.

In 1788 she published *Observations on the New Constitution* in which she expressed her displeasure at what she felt was a betrayal of republican ideals. As an anti-Federalist she opposed its ratification, specifically citing the lack of a Bill of Rights as a major problem. It would be rectified three years later, but Warren was forever disappointed in after years with what she felt was too centralized a federal government.

In 1805 Warren completed her three-volume master work, *A History of the Rise, Progress, and Termination of the American Revolution*. This was no after-thought. It was always her intention and she began writing the first female-authored account of the era back in 1765 when the Stamp Act was defeated. President Thomas Jefferson ordered copies for himself and his cabinet and wrote "*her truthful and insightful account of the last thirty years will furnish a more instructive lesson to mankind than any equal period known in history.*" Her treatment of John Adams however, (whom she believed had been corrupted by his elevation to the heights of political power) led to a series of recriminatory letters between the two and a breach in their friendship which lasted until 1812.

Mercy Otis Warren died on October 19, 1814, at the age of 86 and is buried in Plymouth. A bronze statue of her stands outside the Courthouse in Barnstable County, her birthplace.

No Mercy from Mercy by Melody Brooks

Mercy Otis Warren's unexpected education uncorked, if not a genie then arguably a genius of the literary arts. She produced an enormous amount of writing. In addition to her plays and 1,300 page history of the revolution, there are dozens and dozens of letters and poems written to and sometimes at the behest of, a number of the most prominent men and women engaged in the cause of revolution. Warren's own engagement went beyond the written word. She hosted these leaders at her home in Plymouth where political strategy was discussed and determined and she contributed liberally to the conversations. When she talked, men listened. Among the surviving letters are many from the most prominent people of the day seeking Mercy's opinion and advice, or praising her literary talents.

John Adams took a particular interest in Warren, encouraging her to use her facility with verse to benefit their shared cause. She obliged. Combining her knowledge of classical history with a flair for the theatrical, she composed a series of dramatic satires: *The Adulateur*, *The Defeat*, *The Group*, *The Blockheads*, that she published anonymously in the patriotic press. It would have been foolhardy for her to publish this material under her own name, even if she were not a woman. These were no-holds-barred attacks on prominent supporters of Crown policy, most notably Massachusetts Bay Colony Governor Thomas Hutchinson, for whom she had a particular loathing, believing (as did many of her compatriots) that he had betrayed his American birth for the prospect of personal advancement. Hutchinson is thinly disguised as "Rapatio" of "Upper Servia" in the first of these satires, *The Adulateur*; is killed off in *The Defeat* and referenced again in *The Group*.

The satirical farce was a popular dramatic form of the time and Warren wielded her pen like a knife. Although modern audiences might have trouble following the classical allusions and matching the play's characters to the local personages being skewered, Warren's contemporaries would have known exactly what was being communicated. After publishing *The Group* in 1775, she seemed to fear that she had gone too far. Both John and Abigail Adams reassured her. He noted that "...The business of satyr is to expose vice and vicious men as such to this scorn..." And from Abigail, "I observe my friend is laboring under apprehension, lest the severity with which a certain Group was drawn, was incompatible with that benevolence which ought always to be predominant in a female character...satire in the hands of some is a very dangerous weapon; yet...when truth is unavoidably preserved, and ridiculous and vicious actions are alone the subject, it is so far from blamable that it is certainly meritorious."

Warren sent *The Group* in sections to her husband who it seems, had commissioned it! He didn't keep it to himself, writing on January 15, 1775 to John Adams: "Inclosed are for your amusement two Acts of a dramatic performance composed at my particular desire. They go to you as they came out of the hand of the Copier, without pointing or marking. If you think it worth while to make any other use of them than a reading, you will prepare them in that way & give them such other Corrections & Amendments as your good Judgment shall suggest."

John Adams did indeed think it worthwhile and the play was published in January 1775 in the *Boston Gazette* and the *Massachusetts Spy.* Montrose J. Moses in a 1918 collection of early American plays claims it was published "on the day before the Battle of Lexington" but in a letter to Adams in 1814 Warren reminds him that he "committed it to press the winter before Lexington battle." Moses is referring to the pamphlet version printed in Boston that April; the New York and Philadelphia versions contained only the two scenes that appeared in the newspapers. The Boston pamphlet cover attests "As lately Acted and to be Re-Acted to the Wonder of all Superior Intelligences, Nigh Head Quarters at Amboyne." This is the only indication that *The Group* might have been performed at the time it was written (as it was "near headquarters," it is fun to think that perhaps the Continental Army performed it for their own amusement.)

So well did her husband and his friends maintain Warren's anonymity that, long after the Revolution, when she had already published work in her own name, she was required to seek John Adams' help in proving her authorship. She wrote to him on July 10, 1814, only a few months before her death: "My next question, sir, you may deem impertinent. Do you remember who was the author of a little pamphlet entitled, *The Group*? To your hand it was committed by the writer. You brought it forward to the public eye. I will therefore give you my reason for naming it now. A friend of mine, who lately visited the Athenæum, saw it among a bundle of pamphlets, with a high encomium of the author, who, he asserted, was Mr. Samuel Barrett. You can, if you please, give a written testimony contradictory of the false assertion."

Adams responded: "What brain could ever have conceived or suspected Samuel Barrett, Esquire, to have been the author of *The Group*? I could take my Bible oath ... That there was but one person in the world, male or female, who could at that time, have written it; and that person was Madam Mercy Warren, the historical, philosophical, poetical, and satirical consort of the then Colonel, since General, James Warren of Plymouth, sister of the great, but forgotten, James Otis.

In a subsequent letter to Warren, after she had sent him the original Dramatis Personae because he could no longer remember whom all the characters were representing, Adams informed her that he had been to the Athenæum (a library in Boston), and written down the original names of the people satirized. This copy is still in the possession of the library.

The two plays included in her 1790 collection eschew the satirical and use Warren's classical knowledge to draw analogies to the American Revolution, and in particular to highlight women—virtuous, republican women at least—in the role of revolutionaries and activists. She apparently hadn't lost her touch, receiving a letter from Alexander Hamilton dated July 1st, 1791: "It is certain that in the 'Ladies of Castile', the sex will find a new occasion of triumph. Not being a poet myself, I am in the less danger of feeling mortification at the idea that in the career of dramatic composition at least, female genius in the United States has outstripped the male." With a review like that, it is time to celebrate Mercy Otis Warren as truly the first U.S. female playwright, and not just a useful tool in the propaganda machine of the Revolution.

Democratic Principles are a result of Equality of Condition.
—Mercy Otis Warren

Chicago
by Maurine Dallas Watkins

Directed by **Melody Brooks**
Dramaturgy by **Mari Lyn Henry**
Assistant Director: **Katie McHugh**

Wednesday, December 17, 2014

Maurine Dallas Watkins: Brave Little Woman
by Mari Lyn Henry

Maurine Dallas Watkins (1896-1969) was born in Louisville, Kentucky and began writing as a young girl—producing plays, founding her high school newspaper, and writing short stories. The only child of a Protestant minister, she attended several colleges before landing at Radcliffe where she pursued but did not complete a doctoral degree in the classics. She applied and was accepted into English Professor George Pierce Baker's playwriting workshop at Harvard University. Baker encouraged students to seek experience in the larger world and may have recommended newspaper reporting.

Watkins moved to Chicago in early 1924 and landed a job with the *Chicago Tribune* as a crime reporter. She remained at the paper for seven months covering the murder trials of Belva Gaertner and Beulah Annan. Her articles focused on the farcical, cynical, and sensational aspects of the two cases, the press and public interest, and the legal proceedings—two attractive "jazz babies" claiming to be corrupted by men and liquor. She characterized Beulah as the "beauty of the cell block" and Belva as "most stylish of Murderess Row." Although both women were found not guilty, Watkins was convinced they were. In her reporting, Watkins had cleverly twinned the two murders together. Under a picture of the pair of the accused murderesses captioned "Killers of Men," she wrote that "as yet the two have not talked over their common interests. A man, a woman, liquor and a gun."

She subsequently returned to school to study again under Baker who had moved to Yale. As a class assignment in his famous 47 Workshop course, she wrote a thinly fictionalized account of the two murders, calling it first *The Brave Little Woman*, then *Chicago, or Play Ball* and finally *Chicago*. Beulah became Roxie Hart; Belva Gaertner, Velma Kelly, Albert Annan, Amos Hart and the two lawyers William Scott Stewart and W. W. O'Brien, were combined in a composite character, Billy Flynn.

Professor Baker sent her play (which received an A in his class) to producer Sam Harris in New York, a former business partner of George M. Cohan. Harris, in turn, hired George Abbott to direct *Chicago* on Broadway where it ran for 172 performances during the 1926-27 season and was named as one of the Top Ten plays by leading critic Burns Mantle. On December 31, 1926, Brooks Atkinson, theatre critic for the *New York Times* commented: "*When Roxie Hart, the chief strumpet of this comedy, faces the police and the District Attorney after the murder, she naturally fears the worst. Miss Watkins has striven to show by the method of satire, why no beautiful woman need quail before justice.*" In his preface to the only published edition of the play, eminent critic George Jean Nathan believed that in spite of a few unavoidable defects "*her play is an eminently worth-while affair, its roots in verity, its surface polished with observation and humorous comprehension, its whole witty, wise and appropriately mordant. It is American to the core; there is not a trace of imitativeness in it; and it discloses, unless I am badly mistaken, a talent that will go a considerable distance in the drama of the land.*"

Within a year, *Chicago* was produced as a silent film, supervised by Cecil B. DeMille. It was also the basis for a 1942 film adaptation *Roxie Hart*, starring Ginger Rogers. After it closed on Broadway, it toured for two years with a then unknown Clark Gable appearing in a Los Angeles production as Albert Annan (Amos Hart).

Following *Chicago*'s success, Broadway producers pursued Watkins for new works but those plans didn't materialize. She adapted Samuel Hopkins Adams' book *Revelry*, about the Teapot Dome scandal that tainted the presidency of Warren G. Harding, into a stage play called *Revelry*. She lampooned the ethically-challenged administration of an incompetent, poker-playing and liquor-swilling president. The play touched a raw nerve; *Revelry's* pre-Broadway, out-of-town run was forced to close down in Philadelphia on the charge of being "inimical to the interest of the United States Government" and its Broadway run ended after 48 performances in the 1927-28 season.

She continued to write short stories and other plays including *Gesture, Tinsel Girl, So Help Me God* (which did not premiere until 2009 at the Mint Theater in NYC) and *The Devil's Diary*. Watkins went west to write screenplays including the 1936 Oscar-nominated comedy *Libeled Lady* with William Powell, Myrna Loy, Jean Harlow and Spencer Tracy as well as the screenplay that would be Humphrey Bogart's film acting debut, Fox's *Up the River* (1930) directed by John Ford. She also won acclaim for her screwball comedy, RKO's *Professional Sweetheart* (1933) starring Ginger Rogers.

Watkins faded into obscurity in the 1940s. She moved to Florida, became a born-again Christian and left her fortune of over $2.3 million to found contests and endow Chairs in classical and biblical Greek at a number of universities. Before her death in 1969, she was approached by Bob Fosse who sought the rights to *Chicago* for a musical adaptation but she resisted his offers. There is some speculation that her refusal was influenced by her belief that she helped two murderesses get acquitted. After Watkins' death her estate sold him the rights, leading to the development of *Chicago: A Musical Vaudeville* with a score by Kander and Ebb, first produced in 1975 and still running today.

A Culture of Corruption, Influence, Prohibition
by Mari Lyn Henry

The Roaring Twenties changed Chicago's nickname from 'windy' to 'wicked.' Bathtub gin flowed, bootlegging was a big business, speakeasies were plentiful, the crime bosses under Al Capone oversaw the acquisition of protection fees from small businesses and all liquor distribution. And in the Governor's mansion, Lennington Small, the 26th governor between 1921-1929, was indicted for embezzling $600,000 and running a money laundering scheme when he was State Treasurer. Ironically, he was acquitted but eight jurors got state jobs!

William Hale Thompson, mayor of Chicago from 1915-1923 and then from 1927-1931, was defeated in 1924 by William Emmett Dever. When he ran again in 1927 during a city wide gang war, he held a debate between himself and two live rats he used to portray his opponents. The *Chicago Tribune*, after his final defeat in 1931, wrote that he had "*meant filth, corruption, obscenity and bankruptcy for Chicago. He had given the city an international reputation for moronic buffoonery, barbaric crime, triumphant hoodlumism, unchecked graft, and a dejected citizenship . . . he made Chicago a byword for the collapse of American civilization.*"

But it was also an era when women had won the right to vote and could drive an automobile, lose their corsets and assert their independence from Victorian morality. The flapper could bob her hair or get the marcel wave, a styling technique using hot curling tongs a lá Josephine Baker. She could apply rouge and nail polish, powder from a compact, lipstick from a metal container. Bee stung lips and blush were in vogue. Dark eyes, rimmed in Kohl, were the style. And then there was the popular Black Narcissus perfume created by Caron founder Ernest Daltroff in 1911. Dubbed 'the Film Noir perfume', it expressed a beautiful and dangerous femme fatale, only in it for herself, even though she dresses to 'lure you in.'

The dresses were straight and loose in luxe or lightweight fabrics, leaving bare arms and dropping the waistline to the hips. Skirts rose to just below the knee and some ladies applied rouge to their knees. High heels of two to three inches came into vogue. Large breasts were considered unsophisticated, so women would bind their breasts to achieve the *look*. Silk or rayon stockings were held up by garters.

A short skirt and bobbed hair were considered symbols of emancipation which included premarital sex, birth control, drinking and smoking excessively. Silent screen stars like Louise Brooks and Clara Bow were the poster girls for the flapper. Ann Pennington, the darling with the dimpled knees, was an extremely popular vaudeville star in *The Ziegfeld Follies* and *George White's Scandals* in the 1910s and 1920s. She was renowned for her variation of dancing the Black Bottom and her interpretation of the Charleston.

In 1924, there were eight daily newspapers which covered the scene in Chicago. Over 100 reporters vied for assignments especially when a crime of passion was involved. Robert R. McCormick, the conservative publisher of the *Tribune*, dominated Chicago's morning field and the midwest. Maurine Dallas Watkins was hired to report on major crimes from a woman's perspective. Women were not allowed on juries in the United States at that time. But if you were a pretty woman who wore the appropriate attire and looked remorseful, you were probably not going to hang. Watkins cut her teeth on the Leopold and Loeb Case of 1924 also known as the crime of the century, when the teenaged son of an affluent Jewish family was kidnapped, held for ransom, and murdered, his body found in a culvert near Wolf Lake.

Two murder cases that went viral occurred one month apart. Belva Gaertner, a three-time divorced cabaret singer who used Belle Brown as her professional name, shot and killed her lover Walter Law, a married man with one child on March 11, 1924. He was found sprawled in the front seat of her car with a bottle of gin and a gun lying beside him. She pled amnesia, confessed she was drunk and was driving with him . . . and that she carried a gun for fear of robbers. After her acquittal, she told Ms. Watkins: "No woman can love a man enough to kill him. They aren't worth it, because there are always plenty more. Walter was just a kid. Why should I have worried whether he loved me or left me? Gin and guns—either one is bad enough but together they get you in a dickens of a mess, don't they?"

Beulah Annan shot her lover Harry Kalstedt in the back on April 3, 1924. She sat in the bedroom she shared with her husband drinking and listening to the lyrics of *Hula Lou* on her Victrola—*"I'm a gal that can't be true. I do my dancin' in the evenin' breeze, 'neath the trees I got more sweeties than a dog has fleas"* for at least two hours before she called her husband to tell him about the crime.

There were other women in the Cook County Jail that year and Watkins refers to them in her play. Doug Perry's book *Girls of Murder City: Fame, Lust, and the Beautiful Killers Who Inspired Chicago* (Viking, 2010), describes the rash of forgotten cases which became footnotes. Perry's book explains why Annan and Gaertner were acquitted. They played on the sympathy of the male jurors. Sabella Nitti, described by the *Tribune* as "a cruel animal" after her husband was beaten to death with a hammer, and Kitty Malm, nicknamed Wolf Woman and Tiger Girl after a robbery with her husband went wrong and a security guard was killed, were examples of *rare* convictions. Juries were biased against poor immigrants and verdicts were class based.

Another notorious case involved Wanda Stopa who allegedly tried to shoot the wife of a man she loved, but she ended up killing a handyman at the woman's home. Stopa escaped but before the police could catch her, she swallowed cyanide in a Detroit hotel room. When her family set up her coffin for viewing in their apartment, huge crowds came for a glimpse. Maurine was thunderstruck at how, in death, everybody seemed to love Stopa. It no longer mattered that she had shot and killed an innocent man; it mattered only that her beautiful face and mournful words appeared above the fold of every newspaper in the city. It definitely bothered her that Beulah Annan got off. Watkins wrote *Chicago* as a way of righting that wrong, but she wanted Beulah to be guilty.

Being a conscientious person, I never prayed for a murder, but I hoped if there was one, I'd be assigned to it.

—Maurine Dallas Watkins

Sex
by Mae West

Directed by **Aneesha Kudtarkar**
Dramaturgy by **Celia Braxton**

Wednesday, June 18, 2014

Ahead of the Curve! by Melissa Attebery

Rarely do people think of Mae West as a writer. She's primarily remembered for her voluptuous figure, sexy innuendos and sharp wit, but she was a free-thinking, independent and bold woman long before those qualities became first fashionable, then fundamental. In fact, she was one of the first female American writers, and actors, to demand and receive creative control over her work.

West learned early on that her talent and good looks were an advantage. Her attitudes toward men were heavily influenced by her mother, a former corset and fashion model, who had once idolized performer and suffrage advocate Lillian Russell. West learned to use her sexuality to ally with or dominate men, and she saw marriage as an institution offering legal protection and social acceptance, but robbing women of independence and sexual freedom. She married vaudevillian Frank Wallace in 1911 when she was 17, but kept the marriage a secret, never lived with him and eventually left him without divorcing until 1942. She only admitted to being married to Wallace when she was forced to do so when on trial for her play *Sex* in 1927. She may even have been simultaneously married to musician Guido Deiro, divorcing him in 1920.

Born in Bushwick, Brooklyn in 1893, West started in show business at age 5, entertaining at a church social, and at age 7, billed as "Baby Mae," winning the gold medal in a talent show. It was in Woodhaven, Queens, where West first performed in a bar, Neir's Tavern, which still exists today. Around the age of 13, she began performing on the vaudeville circuit, trying out various personas including a male impersonator, an eccentric country girl and a blackface coon shouter. Her trademark walk may even have been inspired by famous female impersonators during the "Pansy Craze." Soon thereafter, she was performing as the sexy "Baby Vamp," and at 18 she introduced her audiences to the "shimmy," which she'd seen in a nightclub on Chicago's South Side. After her first appearance on Broadway in the 1911 revue *A La Broadway*, West was discovered by the *New York Times*—a "girl named Mae West, hitherto unknown, pleased by her grotesquerie and snappy way of singing and dancing."

With a tremendous wit and intelligence for writing dialogue, West started writing plays and first came to prominence with her production of *Sex*, which was shut down in 1927. West was sentenced to 10 days on Welfare Island (now known as Roosevelt Island) on obscenity charges. It's said that she received star treatment in prison, but she was sympathetic to her less fortunate inmates, and when *Liberty* magazine paid her $1,000 for an exit interview, she used it to start a Mae West Memorial Library for female prisoners.

This instinct to turn injustice into social good was a theme throughout her life, echoing later in the 1930s when one of her many boyfriends, the African American boxing champion William "Gorilla" Jones, was barred by management from entering her apartment building in Los Angeles. West bought the building and lifted the ban.

Her next plays, *The Drag* and *The Pleasure Man*, demonstrated her openness about homosexuality; but it was her 1928 play, *Diamond Lil*, about a racy, easygoing lady of the 1890s, that went from Broadway hit to Hollywood hit. Although she didn't arrive in Hollywood until she was (remarkably) almost 40 years old, she won the respect of Paramount Pictures on the basis of her talent. Unfortunately, the Motion Picture Producers and Distributors of America (commonly known as the Hays Office) had banned *Diamond Lil* as unsuitable for the screen. So, in 1933, West and Paramount made some changes and released the film as *She Done Him Wrong*. It was a huge success, garnering an Academy Award nomination for Cary Grant and saving Paramount from bankruptcy. Under the strict Motion Picture Production Code, West became an expert at evading the censors. She loaded future scripts with obvious material for them to cut, while slipping in double entendres that they would overlook.

Ultimately, West's style was too much for Hollywood, and she turned back to the stage for the next few decades. She re-affirmed her stardom performing in Las Vegas in the 1950s and maintained her strong sexual identity well into her 60s. When the sexual revolution of the 1960s and '70s finally echoed the sentiments West had been championing for 50 years, West experienced a resurgence in popularity and was featured in the 1969 edition of *Life* magazine. A master at reinventing herself, she never stopped asserting her power as an artist and sex symbol, always insisting on playing a woman in her 20s. In 1980, after struggles with diabetes and other ailments, she suffered a series of strokes and died at age 87 in Los Angeles.

For us, West is remembered as more than just the "come up and see me sometime girl." She was an early supporter of the women's liberation movement, an early supporter of gay rights and wrote the urtext for Madonna and Lady Gaga. West once said, "You may admire a girl's curves on the first introduction, but the second meeting shows up new angles." Indeed she showed us new angles—repeatedly breaking barriers of gender and sexuality over an 80+ year career as a writer, performer, free-speech agent and entertainment entrepreneur.

Sex and Scandal: "Queer Fear" on Broadway, 1926 by Celia Braxton

SEX, by Mae West, is best known for two things. First, it was written and produced by the film queen of sexual irony and camp; and second, it was shut down by the police, with Ms. West and the rest of the cast carted off to jail.

According to Marybeth Hamilton in her article, "Mae West Live," West often said the play was shut down because Broadway and its supporters could not handle discussion of sex as an activity, that the word "sex" had not before been used in the newspapers to indicate anything other than what we today would call "gender," and that no newspaper would accept advertisements for the play using its actual title.

In fact, *SEX was* regularly advertised under its own name in mainstream newspapers. The play ran for nearly a year before it was closed down. Nor was it the only play on Broadway that season or for several seasons past that dealt with sex or prostitution. The controversy around Mae West's *SEX* was part of the culture war that roiled around jazz, homosexuality, and the nature of American theatre during the 1920s.

David Savran has pointed out in *Highbrow/Lowdown*, how ubiquitous jazz was during the 1920s, not just on radio, or in cabarets, speakeasies, and vaudeville, but in Broadway musicals as well. Broadway critics and playwrights during the 1920s, however, were entangled in a post-colonial attempt to create an American theatre that would measure up to the Europeans'. Jazz, suddenly always everywhere, elided boundaries of class and culture. As playwright J. Hartley Manners described it, "bodies writhe and intermingle and brains rattle in skulls as the ghastly jigging procession circles under blazing lights to the cheap deafening 'music'(!) of the tire-less orchestras." (qtd. in Savran, 5). Because of jazz, the difference between highbrow and lowbrow sensibilities was no longer clear.

In *SEX*, jazz plays a large part. Act Two, Scene One ostensibly takes place in Trinidad, but actually recreates a New York nightclub, complete with contemporaneous jazz numbers and Mae West doing the shimmy. *SEX* brings jazz and its "ghastly jigging procession" on stage literally, unapologetically situating sex for money squarely within the East Coast white establishment. Two successful prostitute dramas on Broadway that season carefully removed their (non-white) heroines from New York, to Shanghai or Paris. In both plays, the prostitute pays the price of her fall. But West's Margy LaMont, a working class white woman, brings it home. She starts in the rough world of Montreal's red-light district as an entrepreneur selling sex for money, with plans for business growth. Mae West, through LaMont, brings the "shimmy" to the Broadway dramatic stage with the authority of the burlesque performer Mae West had no doubt been for the previous five years. The character ends up in Westchester county and - spoiler alert! - she does not die.

Hamilton argues that *SEX* was West's "last-ditch effort to gain mainstream Broadway success." There is evidence that she was working in burlesque between 1921 and 1926. West had worked in burlesque in her late teens, but by the 1920s, the genre had become rougher and much more identified with pornographic sex than before World War I. Robert C. Allen, in *Horrible Prettiness*, describes early-1920s burlesque featuring striptease in the fight to maintain its working class male audience in the face of cheap movie prices. Film scholar Jon Tuska has presented evidence that West was not only working in burlesque, but on the lowest "wheel" or circuit, of burlesque. The Mutual Wheel ran explicitly sexual shows, with coochie, or shimmy dancing, strip tease, and quite possibly prostitution activities by many of the performers.

The *Herald Tribune* called *SEX* an "exhibition of complete frankness...not sex, but lust—stark, naked lust." "She cavorts her own sex about the stage in one of the most reviling exhibits allowed public display," said the *Daily Mirror*. "She undresses before the public, and appears to enjoy doing so." A scene in the last act, with the stage directions "they kiss," and "they kiss again," is described by the *Times* as "a torrid love scene," a reaction hinted at by other reviewers. Critics generally reacted as though West had brought a real brothel on stage. Perhaps she knew whereof she spoke.

But this is not why *SEX* was closed by the police 41 weeks after it opened. As a 1928 *Times* article, "The Story of Mae West," states, *SEX* became quite a fad, with many of the best people seeing it two or three times. And it was cleared by a "functioning play jury" in the summer of 1926. No. *SEX* was actually closed to prevent West opening her next show, *The Drag*.

The Drag tells the story of a wealthy young man of prominent family who marries to hide his homosexual nature. The plot follows the result of this deception on his family and his personal life, leading finally to his murder. Descriptions of the rehearsal process make it clear that *The Drag* was what we now call devised theatre - at least partially. Sixty young men were chosen from a crowd of auditioners solicited at a gay nightclub. Rehearsals for *The Drag* were improvisations aimed at capturing real language and mannerisms, while creating two authentic party scenes for the play. (Hamilton) This authenticity was what had been so successful in gaining an audience for *SEX*.

The presence on Broadway of the growing gay subculture, using actual gay performers who were encouraged to exaggerate their more outrageous behavior on stage, might have left Broadway exposed to the raunchiest burlesque, then relegated to the city borders...changed the audience mix...destroyed the economics of an important and thriving industry! If successful, *The Drag* would have destabilized the fragile developing highbrow/middlebrow theatrical mystique!

The theatrical establishment and anti-vice communities came together quickly in early 1927. The Wales Padlock Act banned any depiction of gay or lesbian love on stage. Theatres housing such performances could be padlocked for up to a year. On February 9, 1927, after several riotous previews of *The Drag* in New Haven and Newark, *SEX* and two other plays—both on homosexual themes—were closed down. *The Drag* was locked out of the city. But within a year, Mae West had figured out that making fun of the censors would get her farther, faster, than sex itself.

When choosing between two evils, I always like to try the one I've never tried before.
—Mae West

Women of Provincetown Players
The Rescue by Rita Creighton Smith
The Widow's Veil by Alice L. Rostetter
Aria da Capo by Edna St. Vincent Millay
Directed by **Elysa Marden**
Dramaturgy by **Shana Komitee**
Wednesday, May 21, 2014

Meet the Writers by Melody Brooks

The best known and most prolific of the writers in this program is poet and playwright **Edna St. Vincent Millay.** She was born in Rockland, Maine on February 22, 1892. Her mother, Cora, raised her three daughters on her own after asking her husband to leave in 1899. She encouraged her girls to be ambitious and self-sufficient, teaching them an appreciation of music and literature from an early age. In 1912, Millay entered her poem "Renascence" into a contest: she won fourth place and publication in *The Lyric Year*, bringing her immediate acclaim and a scholarship to Vassar College. There, she continued to write poetry and became involved in the theater. In 1917, the year of her graduation, Millay published her first book, *Renascence and Other Poems.* At the request of Vassar's drama department, she also wrote her first verse play, *The Lamp and the Bell* (1921), a work about love between women.

After graduation Millay moved to Greenwich Village, living in a house owned by the Cherry Lane Theatre at 75½ Bedford St, renowned for being the smallest in New York City. She joined the Provincetown Players in its early days and critic Floyd Dell wrote that the red-haired and beautiful Millay was "a frivolous young woman, with a brand-new pair of dancing slippers and a mouth like a valentine." Millay, who was openly bisexual, described her life in New York as "very, very poor and very, very merry." She published *A Few Figs from Thistles* (1920), a volume of poetry which drew much attention for its controversial descriptions of female sexuality and feminism. In 1923 her fourth volume of poems, *The Harp Weaver*, was awarded the Pulitzer Prize—she was the third woman to be so honored. In addition to publishing three plays in verse, Millay also wrote the libretto of one of the few American grand operas, *The King's Henchman* (1927).

Millay married Eugene Boissevain, a self-proclaimed feminist and widower of Inez Milholland, in 1923. Boissevain gave up his own pursuits to manage Millay's literary career, setting up the readings and public appearances for which Millay grew quite famous. According to Millay's own accounts, the couple acted liked two bachelors, remaining "sexually open" throughout their twenty-six-year marriage, which ended with Boissevain's death in 1949. Millay herself died the next year. On her death, *The New York Times* described her as "an idol of the younger generation during the glorious early days of Greenwich Village [. . .] One of the greatest American poets of her time." Thomas Hardy said that America had two great attractions: the skyscraper and the poetry of Edna St. Vincent Millay.

In contrast, we have **Alice L. Rostetter**, a high school English teacher for whom *The Widow's Veil* was an anomaly. Rostetter was better known for her children's plays and *Veil* appears to be the only script for adults she produced. Born in New York City, Rostetter graduated from Hunter College in 1899 and taught at Washington Irving High School for years before *The Widow's Veil* opened at the Provincetown Players on January 17, 1919. One of her students was Lily Claudetter Chauchoin, who had moved with her family from France to New York in 1910. She became known to the world as Claudette Colbert, and although the evidence is inconclusive, would later claim to have made her stage debut, at her teacher's urging, in the *Widow's Veil.*

Veil was unequivocally among the most successful of the Provincetown plays, called "the hit of the bill" upon which it first appeared, and went on to be produced again and again in different programs, including the Review Bill of 1919 (the "best of" the season.) Critical response was uniformly positive, sometimes effusive. *The Morning Telegraph* praised Rostetter's acting as well as her writing, and found *Veil* the best of the four works presented. Noted drama critic Heywood Broun claimed that *The Widow's Veil* was "the best-one-act play we have seen in two seasons and among the most notable achievements of the interesting organization in Macdougal Street." The play was published by Egmont Arens in 1920 in the "Flying Stag Plays for the Little Theatre" series, reprinted in the Provincetown Plays volume edited by George Cram Cook and Frank Shay in

1921, and was re-mounted by the Players in the "unofficial" spring season of 1921 along with *Aria da Capo* and Gustav Wied's *Autumn Fires*.

Rostetter worked with the Players as an actor for three seasons, performing her last role in Eugene O'Neill's *Diff'rent* in December 1920. In 1925 she appeared in the Experimental Theatre's production of *A Dream Play*. She did continue to write for young audiences, and in 1927 was a delegate to the National Conference on the Theatre at Yale University. But there is no evidence that she wrote any more plays for adults. Rostetter disappears from the public record after 1927, but there is a NY Times obituary for Alice L. Rostetter who died May 16, 1961.

Creighton Smith at 11 years old

Rita Creighton Smith is the least known (and knowable) of these writers. She appears to have been born on October 6, 1877 in Thomaston, Maine, granddaughter to a prominent sea captain and ship builder. Little of her life before moving to New York is easily found, but it appears from Library of Congress records that she submitted plays as early as 1909, with the last of her dramatic works copyrighted in 1923. She wrote about a dozen plays; most were never published or produced. Smith was a student in George Pierce Baker's famous English 47 Workshop at Radcliffe in 1915-16. She maintained a relationship with him afterwards—it is through correspondence with Baker that we know much of what is available about her writing. Judith Barlow, in *Women Writers of the Provincetown Players*, considers Smith's full-length dramas formulaic and too concerned with achieving a commercial production.

The Rescue is an exception to this cookie-cutter approach (as it was also for The Provincetown Players which generally produced only new work.) First performed by the Harvard Dramatic Club on April 11 and 12, 1916, this short play addresses a number of provocative issues for the time. Critical response was mixed, but the *New York Herald* found it "an interesting psychological drama..." Although this was the only play by Smith that the Players produced, there is speculation from multiple sources that she may have had a substantial influence on other Provincetown writers, especially Eugene O'Neill. It is felt that he might have borrowed the theme of inherited insanity for *Strange Interlude* (1928); and several of the ideas relating to inheritance and their visual realization on stage in *Mourning Becomes Electra* (1931). If this is so then, although largely unknown herself, Smith's lasting legacy may well be embedded within these two classics of the American Canon.

Ladies First: Women's Leading Role in the Provincetown Players
by Shana Komitee

Ninety years before an American woman first clinched a major-party nomination for U.S. president, forty-five years before Betty Friedan's The Feminine Mystique sparked the modern feminist movement, and five years before American women even possessed the legal right to vote, female artists had already taken center stage at the Provincetown Players. Founded on Cape Cod, Massachusetts by a small group of friends in the summer of 1915, the Players sought to offer an artistic and spiritual alternative to Broadway—to provide, as their leading visionary George Cram Cook put it, "an oasis in the desert of uninspired commercial theater offerings in America." They ran for seven years, produced nearly a hundred new plays by fifty American playwrights, and gave birth to at least two dramatic giants along the way—Eugene O'Neill and Susan Glaspell.

Many people know about the Provincetown Players' contribution to non-profit American theater—their literary and ideological achievements are well-documented and widely celebrated. Yet less well-known is the defining role of women in the group. While in the commercial theater world opportunities for women playwrights, directors, and producers were often limited, Provincetown's female members easily adopted and excelled in each of these capacities. In many ways they were the backbone of this revolutionary theater group. Few of the American female playwrights we now consider canonical—Lorraine Hansberry, Adrienne Kennedy, Maria Irene Fornés—were even born, let alone writing plays, when Provincetown's progressive women took the helm.

Tonight we will look at three plays by women in the group: Alice Rostetter's *The Widow's Veil*; Rita Creighton Smith's *The Rescue*; and Edna St. Vincent Millay's *Aria da Capo*. The works all premiered between 1918-1920, have female protagonists, and explore issues endemic to women's experience. In *The Widow's Veil*, for instance, the characters are all women (except for an unaccommodating male janitor whom we do not see). Some are out of sight, but their voices are still heard: there's a (possibly lesbian?) couple on the sixth floor of the building; an unhappy mother of a colicky baby across the hall; and others. The primary focus, though, is on the intergenerational friendship between the young Katy MacManus and her would-be mentor, Mrs. Phelan. The two meet daily in the private space between their apartments to commiserate about—then strategize how to handle—the apparent impending death of Katy's husband, merely ten days after her marriage. We all recognize the structure of their girl-talk: Katy laments her plight, and Mrs. Phelan offers her hard-earned wisdom. Their heated conversations, though frequently hilarious to us, are a lifeline for both women.

The play's power derives from the way Rostetter embeds the women's dialogue with a radically "feminist" question, even before that term circulated widely in America. Would perhaps widowhood, not marriage, finally allow Katy to see herself as beautiful, independent, self-regarding? The play's answer seems to be yes—that is, if Katy can wear the lovely widow's veil Mrs. Phelan has preemptively secured for her. When Katy must demur the offer because Mr. MacManus's health has improved, we're forced to consider the play's paradoxical suggestion: being a wife seems to mean subservience to a demanding husband—a kind of death; whereas being widowed would have promised beauty—a kind of birth. While Rostetter had to soften the play's subversive edge with playful humor, smart audiences nonetheless heard its bite. *The Widow's Veil* became popular throughout America, and traveled to Little Theaters across the country for years following its premiere. To this day, it provides a window into the daring, funny, deeply honest look at marriage that Rostetter, her female characters, and the Player's actresses pushed to the fore.

Our three playwrights didn't limit themselves to subjects most women were expected to relate to—courtship, marriage, motherhood. In *The Rescue*, Smith ventures deeper into the taboo (for the time) fact of mental illness, and the challenge it presents to a young woman whose family is burdened by it. In the play, Anna Warden confronts—and ultimately frees herself from—the Puritanical, "life-denying" yoke of her father's depressive lineage. With the help of her forward-looking maternal aunt, Anna escapes from her cloistered home to take a new job as a single woman in New York City. At the end of the play, she cries out with elation: "I'm not a Warden at all! I—I—am not—a Warden! And I've let you draw a net around me . . . . [But] I am not a Warden! . . . Let me pass, please!" Smith wrote of a courageous woman venturing into unchartered territories- just as she, the playwright, was doing the same with this brave work.

Edna St. Vincent Millay's *Aria da Capo* is commonly seen as an anti-war parody, depicting how fast a seemingly innocent game between men can escalate to diehard competition, then total destruction. Yet Millay also offers within the play a poignant critique of female-male relationships. In her extensive explanatory notes, she explains the sad truth of her male and female character's interaction: "She [Columbine] bores him [Pierrot] to death." Millay tells us the girl could have been different, had she not so desperately sought male approval: "Her expression, 'I cannot live without' this or that, is a phrase she uses in order to make herself more attractive, because she believes men prefer women to be useless and extravagant; if left to herself she would be a domestic and capable person." Millay exposed the dangerous "dumbing down" women often subject themselves to in order to appear more desirable to the opposite sex.

But the real daring of this play is its structural ambition. Millay creates an exciting mélange of styles: *Aria da Capo* is a bucolic pastoral, bookended by a harlequinade, with both realistic and Commedia dell'arte elements. It contains dialogue and staging that can't be pinned down: it's playful but piercing; delicate but deadly. At this time in European history, men were largely the ones experimenting with such modernist collage forms (think Picasso and the Cubists, Strindberg, Jarry, et al.). Yet Millay put the lie to the idea that women couldn't be equally provocative. She began and ended her play with exactly the same words twenty years before Thorton Wilder did the same in *The Skin of Our Teeth*. She used an intricate "double-play" format fifty years before Tom Stoppard did so in *Rosencrantz and Guildenstern Are Dead*. Millay didn't simply hold her own with her male peers. She was ahead of the curve.

And by shaping *Aria da Capo* cyclically, Millay also rejected the still pervasive 19th-century recipe for a "well-made" play. As she saw it, a play need not—indeed should not—build to a tidy linear climax. Perhaps a female dramatist was best suited to state this truth. No conclusive answer to humanity's deepest questions—of love, sexuality, spirituality, and death—can be achieved within a mere two hours at the theater. But gifted playwrights, like the three women whose works are presented tonight, can point the way.

I am glad that I paid so little attention to good advice; had I abided by it I might have been saved from some of my most valuable mistakes.

—Edna St. Vincent Millay

The Suffragists
Lady Geraldine's Speech by Beatrice Harraden
How the Vote Was Won by Cicely Hamilton and Christopher St. John
Mother's Meeting by Mrs. Harlow Phibbs

Directed by **Melissa Attebery**
Dramaturgy by **Barbara Cohen-Stratyner**
Assistant Director: **Kristin Heckler**

Wednesday, February 18, 2015

Meet the Suffragists by Barbara Cohen-Stratyner

The British Suffrage movement believed that 1910 was a tipping point in the fight for voting rights equal to those for men. The Women's Social and Political Union was negotiating with politicians from all three parliamentary parties and felt that victory would come soon. The local and professionally-based suffrage organizations throughout the British Isles (and North America) rallied to provide popular support and funds. Among the most effective were the intertwined Actress Franchise League and Women Writers' Suffrage League. Working together, they developed a portfolio of plays for what later American feminists would call consciousness- and fund-raising. Some were reinterpretations, such as Adeline Bourne's 1910 feminist production of Oscar Wilde's *Salome*. But most of the events featured new plays, ranging from pageants to monologues and represent the work of professional writers united by their belief in women's rights. They were published and distributed by the organizations, although some were also published in acting editions for general use. Many of the performers associated with the plays had transatlantic careers and reputations. So, as well as the British productions, at least one triple bill of Actress Franchise League plays, featuring *How the Vote was Won*, was presented in North America, appearing in New York, Philadelphia and Chicago, 1910-1911.

Beatrice Harraden (1864-1936) was a popular writer, best known for her romantic novels. A graduate of Bedford College, the University of London, she was as well educated as possible for a Victorian woman, in common with the accomplished characters that she created in *Lady Geraldine's Speech*. Harraden was active in the Women Writers' Suffrage League and the Women's Social and Political Union, and wrote extensively for the newspaper *Votes for Women*, which is mentioned in two of the plays. As an author of successful novels, including the best-selling tragic romance *Ships That Pass* (1893), she earned a large, discretionary income. So she was also an active member of the Women's Tax Resistance League, demanding equal property rights and no taxation without representation.

Mrs. Harlow Phibbs (1864-1932) poked fun at herself as the "vicar's wife," running Mothers Meetings. Her husband was a Church of England (Anglican) minister in Hastings, Sussex (south England, near the Channel). She was active in regional Suffrage movements. Her 1912 play *The Rack* was reviewed as a "merry trifle" on a triple bill of Actress Franchise League plays in London (February 1912). Naomi Paxton, Actress Franchise League scholar and editor of the *Methuen Drama Book of Suffrage Plays*, suggests that she was Frances Lina Stanley Phibbs, who wrote the 1901 Suffrage monologue *Jim's Leg*.

Cicely Hamilton (b. Cicely Hammill, 1872-1952) co-founded the Women Writers' Suffrage League with Bessie Hatton (whose play *Before the Dawn* appeared on the Actress Franchise League's New York matinee program). Her *Diana of Dobson's* was a popular social comedy, premiered in 1909 and frequently revived. As well as today's play, she co-wrote *A Pageant of Great Women* with its director Edith Craig (1909) and the lyrics for the Suffrage anthem "March of the Women" (to music by Ethel Smyth), 1910. Primarily a non-fiction writer, her later credits include *The Old Vic* (co-written with its director Lillian Baylis) and the series *Modern [country] as Seen by an Englishwoman* (1931-1939). Like Actress Franchise League founder Adeline Bourne, she turned her Suffrage organizing skills to service during World War I and was honored as a founder of troop entertainment (similar to the USO).

Christopher St.John (b. Christabel Marshall, 1871-1960) was active in both creative Suffrage organizations. Her *How the Vote was Won* is a domestic farce. But she is better remembered for her translations and editing of European experimental theater for the Pioneer Players, managed by her partner, the director and designer Edith Craig, in the 1910s and 1920s. St. John also edited the correspondence of George Bernard Shaw with Craig's mother, famed actress Ellen Terry (1931), as well as her *Lectures on Shakespeare* (1932) and *Memoirs* (1933).

Although not credited as a playwright here, **Edith Craig** served as producer/director of most of the Suffrage plays. The daughter of Ellen Terry and architect E. W. Godwin, she acted in the Lyceum company and in new plays, most notably creating the role of Prossy in Shaw's *Candida* (1900). She also worked in design, costume construction, and stage management. Craig directed and presented over 150 plays, as well as pageants and films. She founded the Pioneer Players in 1911, and also directed for the Everyman Theatre, Hampstead, a hotbed of London's experimental Little Theatre movement.

Plays about Speeches by Barbara Cohen-Stratyner, Ph.D.

In the years of the Actress Franchise League performances, 1909-1911, attaining Suffrage equal to men seemed possible. The various leagues and committees focused on working within the system, gaining support with members of the 3 major parties for incremental changes to property, custody and voting laws. But, this strategy failed and the cause became more and more segmented. The Actress Franchise League maintained neutrality, but the optimism of the 1909-1911 plays faded.

These plays are well constructed with opportunities for performers to make an impact with only a few lines. *The Mothers' Meeting* is a tour de force of dialect humor; the other two plays are farces, filling a room with a social situation gone wrong, accumulating characters, each making an entrance in turn.

The audience was generally sympathetic to the cause, so the purpose of plays was to promote active participation and, of course, raise funds through ticket, programme and ribbons sales. Rather than preaching or showing ways of political persuading, they focus on ways of learning. The sympathetic characters are the audience stand-ins, gaining understanding of the need for equal suffrage. Lady Geraldine and the two husbands in *How the Vote was Won* see the light and are welcomed by the other characters and the audience into the cause.

Two forms of active participation are important to these plays. Characters in two of them enter proclaiming success at selling newspapers. This was usually the first political activity, similar to modern-day distributing flyers and selling buttons. In 1909-1910, Suffragists sold *Votes for Women*, founded as a monthly in 1907, but a weekly after 1908. The newspaper covered the activities of regional and professional groups, and provided almost daily coverage of political and Parliamentary proceedings concerning women's rights. The newspaper also ran advertisements for friendly firms (such as Women's driving schools) and events. By 1910, the circulation was 30,000 per week, primarily from individual sales.

The other active participation that concerns the plays' characters is making a speech. Proclaiming your political beliefs in public was definitely not covered by the Edwardian etiquette books, which were just edging out of the "seen and admired, but not heard" era. For the political women on both sides of the issues, it was a major achievement—an accomplishment of both political clarity and sheer nerve.

Lady Geraldine has been manipulated into giving an Anti-Suffrage speech so she guilts an old school friend into writing it for her, even though Dr. Alice is an active Suffragist. Since this happens during her "at home," additional Suffragist avatars of accomplishment and clear thinking make their entrances and converse, assuming that Geraldine is one of them. This fellowship, rather than political lecturing, persuades her to change her views. Staying within character, she doesn't immediately offer to give a suffrage speech, but announces plans to avoid giving the anti-Suffrage one.

In *The Mothers Meeting*, the speaker has been invited to a Mothers Meeting by the vicar's wife, but goes into the wrong hall, where she interrupts an Anti-Suffrage speech. Her refutation of its errors segues into her own talk and she receives an invitation to give the lecture at a later date. This monologue also represents an effort to present Suffrage as a cause for all women, not just the professionals or educated ones. It uses malperceptions, hearing words as inappropriate, such as "the woman's fear is the home" and "no credit to their sects" although she didn't say if they were Chapel..." The puns emphasize the errors in the original quotes—"women's sphere is the home" lasted long enough to inspire the t-shirt slogan that a woman's place is in the house... and in the senate. As the play progresses, she provides biographical information of her late husband and accomplished children, while complaining about unequal pay.

Originated in mid-19th century urban mission work, by the 1900s, Mothers' Meetings became the purview of the local Anglican minister's wife, 'the vicar's wife." Lina Stanley Phibbs was a vicar's wife, as was Educational pioneer Henrietta Barnett, who analyzed the phenomenon in 1919 as "The advantage of Mothers' Meetings consists not so much in the actual teaching which is given, nor in the habit of savings which is encouraged, as in the sense of fellowship which is fostered."

How the Vote was Won

Published by Women's Writers' Suffrage League, London, the play was re-published and distributed by Dramatic Publishing (Chicago, 1910), which described it as "Easy English comedy... Lively and clever Suffrage sketch... English atmosphere should be suggested but the effectiveness of the plays does not depend on the local color." It became a reliable fund-raising tool in England and the United States since, as well as propaganda, it is "a capital bit or farcical satire," per the Chicago *Record* April 7, 1911. It is both a drawing room comedy and a farce, setting up a physical and social space, then bringing more and more characters into it. Each performer gets to make a solo entrance, quickly establish a character, and make a political point. Finally, Horace understands and takes his turn at speech-making.

It was the finale of a triple bill of suffrage plays with *Before the Dawn*, set in 1867 London, by Bessie Hatton, *A Woman's Influence* by Gertrude Jennings, and a reading by novelist Charlotte Perkins Gilman. The first presentation, with a transatlantic cast, was given in aid of The Equality League of Self-Supporting Women, for a single matinee on March 31, 1910. It was co-stage managed by Beatrice Forbes-Robertson (who played "Winifred"). She also presented the three plays in Chicago for the benefit of the Illinois Equal Suffrage Association (March 1911) and in Philadelphia (February 16) under the auspices of the Pennsylvania Limited Suffrage League, the Equal Franchise Society of Pennsylvania and the College Equal Suffrage League. The latter's program included the pragmatic statement: "A collection for the benefit of the Suffrage Cause will be taken before the last play. Those who do not wish to give, need not do so, as they have already bought tickets. On the other hand, the audience is asked to remember that the expenses of a Suffrage campaign are very heavy, especially this year, as two Women Suffrage bills are to be presented to the Pennsylvania Legislature and if the Suffragists wish to continue holding meetings and distributing literature they must receive financial support."

Plays were given and funds were raised. The campaign for Suffrage fostered fellowship within the movement and, through Actress Franchise League plays, with the audience.

Different as were our antecedents, our characters, our temperaments, our talents, we belonged to the same world, the artist's world.
        —Christopher St. John, re: her menage a trois relationship with Edith Craig and Clare "Tony" Atwood

How Far Have We Come?
Shattered Nerves by Harriet Louisa Childe-Pemberton
Miss Appleyard's Awakening by Evelyn Glover
An Anti-suffrage Monologue by Marie Jenney Howe

Director/Dramaturg: **Melody Brooks**

Wednesday, December 7, 2016

Lost Treasures **by Melody Brooks**

HARRIET LOUISA CHILDE-PEMBERTON was an English poet, playwright and novelist. She was a member of the Christian Knowledge Society and is most known for writing children's literature according to Christian ideals. Childe-Pemberton was a prolific writer, with books, poems, plays and literary criticism published between 1873 and 1911. Very little is knowable about her life; even her year of birth is not certain. She was born circa 1853 and died in 1922, but other biographical details are elusive.

Childe-Pemberton's writing is, however, cited repeatedly in scholarly works examining fairy tales, especially those that reveal the coded messages for girls and young women in Victorian children's literature. For instance, in her retelling of *Red Riding Hood* (subtitled *All My Doing*), "Pussy, like all traditional heroines of Little Red Riding Hood stories, is responsible for her own downfall and rapaciousness of wolfish creatures. The accusatory tone and moralistic message . . . insisted that girls clean up their act, become doll-like angels, or else receive the punishment they deserve."[1] Perhaps her best-known novel is *Birdie: A Tale of Child Life,* in which a young girl must come to terms with the death of her mother and learn to accept the authority of a stepmother.

All of Childe-Pemberton's writing is similarly moralistic, and yet there is a lurking feminist sentiment as well—especially in the fact that most of her protagonists are independent-minded females. It is hard to know whether this strain was deliberate, or simply a function of the fact that Childe-Pemberton herself was clearly pursuing a non-traditional profession for her gender, and pursuing it vigorously, as evidenced by the body of work she left behind: *The Fairy Tales of Every Day* (1882), *Olive Smith; or, An Ugly Duckling* (1883), *Prince: A Story of the American War and Other Narrative Poems* (1883), *No Beauty* (1884), *Birdie: A Tale of Child-Life* (1888), *A Backward Child* (1890), *Under the Trees* (1890), *Fire and War* (1891), *Dead Letters, and Other Narrative and Dramatic Pieces* (1896), *Twenty Minutes: Drawing-Room Duologues, etc.* (1899), *In a Tuscan Villa and Other Poems* (unknown), *Love Knows and Waits, and Other Poems* (unknown), *Her Own Enemy: A Play* (1905), *Text and Stage Business* (1906), *Nenuphar: The Four-Fold Flower of Life* (1911). Given her prodigious output, and the lack of knowledge about her work, Childe-Pemberton stands as a quintessential example of the effort to reclaim the history of women in theatre!

EVELYN GLOVER, is yet another woman about whom not enough is known, although again, we know that she had a long and successful writing career. She appears to have been born in 1874 in Lancashire in England and began as a playwright contributing several comic, polemical sketches to the suffrage cause. These one-act plays seek to demonstrate the relevance of the suffrage movement to working-class women, unlike many that focused on the gentry. In June, 1911, her first play, *Miss Appleyard's Awakening* was published by the Actresses' Franchise League (AFL). In February 1912, *A Chat with Mrs. Chicky* was performed at the Rehearsal Theatre in London with Inez Bensusan in the title role. Bensusan was a noted Australian actress working in London, Secretary of the AFL, and founder of the Women's Theatre Company in 1913. During the First World War, the AFL sent women to entertain the troops in camps and hospitals; one of Glover's shorts, *A Bit of Blighty,* was highly popular. Other works include *A Question of Time* (1908) co-written with F. Mathias Alexander, *Showin' Samyel* (1914), *Their Mothers* (1917), *Time to Wake Up* (1919) and *Thieves in the Night* (1921). She wrote several short stories for BBC Radio that were broadcast between 1927 and 1934 and a children's series prepared for BBC Radio, *The Careful Queen* (1934-35). In December 1938, Glover published a pseudo biography *Cats and My Camera,* subtitled *Some Mental and Photographic Reflections.* The text consists of clever and entertaining anecdotes about the many cats who had crossed her path along with the humans they "owned," but gives little personal information away. The date of Glover's death is not known, but her correspondence with the Society of Authors is dated in the British Library Manuscript Catalogue 1921-1941. The

National Register of Archives therefore lists her dates as 1911-1941—which merely reflects the facts that her first play, *Miss Appleyard's Awakening,* was produced in 1911, and that her correspondence with the Society ended in 1941. It may or may not mean that she died in 1941.

 MARIE JENNEY HOWE was a fascinating and highly accomplished woman. She was born in Syracuse in 1870 to a noted family. In 1897, she graduated from Union Theological Seminary in PA and took a position in Sioux City, Iowa, as an assistant to Unitarian minister Mary A. Safford, president of the Iowa Suffrage Association. Howe maintained the congregation at Des Moines' First Unitarian Church from 1899 to 1904. But she grew frustrated with her church's lack of enthusiasm for social causes, the drudgery of her work and her treatment as a woman in a male profession.

She married political reformer Frederic C. Howe in 1904. The couple lived in Cleveland, then moved to New York City in 1910 where she helped to form the New York State Suffrage League and became chair of the 25th Assembly District division of the Woman Suffrage Party. She and Fred took up residence in Greenwich Village and interacted with some of the leading bohemians and political activists of the day.

In 1912, she founded what became one of the most important women's institutions in the United States, Heterodoxy. In its early years, membership in the luncheon and debate club grew from twenty-five to sixty and included most of the major female social, political, intellectual, and artistic leaders of the day. The only requirement for membership was that the applicant "not be orthodox in her opinion." During World War I, Heterodoxy was under constant government surveillance and had to move venues for every meeting. In 1918, Howe wrote *Telling the Truth at the White House,* a play about the suffrage march in Washington DC, with Paula O. Jakobi, and then found herself taken into custody by the Secret Service in 1919 and questioned about her radical political activities.

Howe collaborated with many other activists and writers on essays, magazine articles, speeches, and propaganda plays, including at least two with the lesbian writer and editor Rose Emmet Young, her close companion for many years. It is unclear whether Howe had a sexual relationship with Young, but she dedicated her first book to her. In 1926, Howe moved to Paris to research the life of George Sand, publishing a critically acclaimed biography in 1927. Her second book, a translation of Sand's journal, appeared in 1929. By this point, Howe was suffering from heart trouble and spent her final years corresponding with Heterodoxy members. When she died in her sleep in 1934, club members consoled Rose Young, rather than Frederic Howe, and asked her advice for memorial service arrangements. Heterodoxy continued monthly meetings until the early 1940s, by which time many of the original members had also died.

Everything Old Is New Again by Melody Brooks

In choosing our theme for the first OHS presentation of the 2016-2017 season, we were mindful of the historic election underway—the first nomination of a woman by a major party for the office of the President of the United States. Of course, like many of our colleagues and associates, we could not anticipate the shocking outcome, but we were very aware of the blatant misogyny and sexism—long considered to be on the wane or at least tamped down—embedded in the attacks by her opponents and the media coverage of her candidacy. So in the midst of the campaign, we decided go back a century and look at plays by women that were championing the so-called "New Woman" and agitating for increased access to education, the workforce, and the ballot box.

Of the three short plays presented tonight, two are written by English women about whom we know very little, although their work is known. Could there be a better example of accomplished women who have "disappeared" from our theatrical heritage? The third piece is by a pioneering American feminist and suffragist, whose life and work is known (although not by the general public) largely because she founded an important club for women that served as a gathering place for many of the feminist leaders of the early to mid-20th Century.

Although all these women wrote in multiple genres, they each found the theatre to be an effective medium for a political message, a purpose as old as the art itself and one which we still find valuable today (*Hamilton* immediately springs to mind!). Each play makes its case indirectly with perhaps a more "feminine" style of persuasion than an outright demand for change. Each is what we might now consider a "playlet," which allowed the works to be performed for a variety of audiences in venues from private drawing rooms to meeting halls to commercial theatres. They were used to educate, fundraise and recruit, presented solo or as part of a larger bill of entertainment. These three works are just a tiny example of what were hundreds if not thousands of plays by women written and performed from the end of the 19th Century until winning the vote—1920 in the US; 1918 in the UK (for property-owning women over 30); and 1928 for all women over 21.

In *Shattered Nerves*, Harriet Louisa Childe-Pemberton introduces us to a female M.D., although she is still only referred to as Mrs. Piercey-Sharpe. The setting is a consulting room, and Lady Flora, who has been diagnosed with every disability one can think of (and then some!) comes seeking the advice of a female specialist. Childe-Pemberton satirizes the Victorian penchant for churning out lists of symptoms that would signify "Hysteria" (one physician came up with 75 and called his list "incomplete"); she also is taking aim at her upper middle-class peers who succumb to the ministrations of any quack practitioner who charges a high enough fee. It would be difficult for us today to argue with this doctor's prescription—a healthy dose of common sense. The play is part of a collection *Twenty Minutes!: Drawing Room Duologues*, published c1900, which contains seven duologues and two monologues—all of which convey a highly moralistic tone. Yet *Shattered Nerves* is a comic gem, and we can easily substitute some of today's preoccupations with the latest trends in health and beauty for Lady Flora's ridiculous situation.

It is fascinating to note that Childe-Pemberton specifically states in her Preface to *Twenty Minutes!* that she expects to be paid half a guinea for her work (roughly equivalent to today's royalties for a one-act play), and stipulates that no performances may take place without prior written authority from her publisher, Samuel French. She is clearly no amateur, and the professional level of publication given these plays increases the frustration at the lack of more information about this woman.

Miss Appleyard's Awakening is the first play credited to Evelyn Glover, who was very active in the suffrage movement in England. The play is out of the ordinary among suffrage pieces, in that it is an appeal to working women. Although we don't know how Miss Appleyard supports herself, we know that she is single and maintains her own household. But with only two servants (one of whom has an important role in the play), she is clearly not a member of the upper class. She belongs to the Anti-Suffrage Society and has been active in promoting her side's views on national suffrage (she is in favor only of local voting rights for women apparently.) Mrs. Crabtree is a typical depiction of a clueless society matron, who has taken the pronunciations of a woman's "unfitness" for political activity a little too much to heart. Her attempt to secure Miss Appleyard's signature on a petition essentially blacklisting fellow anti-suffragists produces a surprising convert, and Miss Appleyard herself discovers that her servants may be better allies than she had thought. In addition to the plot twist, Glover also is clearly having fun with the naming of her characters, with Appleyard conveying a sense of youth and vibrancy, and Crabtree one of bitterness and futility. Her acronym for the Anti-Suffrage Society is particularly brilliant!

"Anti-suffragists did not deny that women had natural rights, but they pointed to their natural differences in order to deny equal political rights for women. Throughout the United States, four premises supported this denial of equal political rights: that God ordained women to serve the desires of men; that women consented to obey men in exchange for protection, thereby creating an inequality; that women voting would not be able to fulfill their role as the caretaker of the family; and the belief that women are "good persons" which made them ineligible to become "good citizens" since good citizens occasionally have to engage in bad behavior.[1]

In 1912 (the same year she founded Heterodoxy), Marie Jenney Howe wrote An Anti-Suffrage Monologue for the drama group of the New York Woman's Suffrage Party. One of the most widely performed and successful of such scripts, the monologue parodies each of the premises noted above and essentially rips them to shreds. Howe also captures the reality that the leaders of the anti-suffrage movement were from the Upper Classes, who fought the vote for women as a threat to their own positions of privilege. After 1920, the anti-suffragists transformed into the Anti-feminists, who feared that feminist influence would make the newly enfranchised women support radical legislation to expand the role of the state. They believed that such state-expanding measures would be detrimental to the patriarchal family—the cornerstone of their world. It is chilling to note that this is the very same argument we hear today from conservatives and the religious right against expanded civil liberties and social safety-net programs. And we certainly have just seen what happens when a particular segment of the population feels that their privilege is threatened. HOW FAR, INDEED, HAVE WE COME?

---

1. Suzanne M. Marilley, *Woman Suffrage and the Origins of Liberal Feminism in the United States, 1820-1920* (Cambridge: Harvard University Press, 1996), 4.

Besides, when I look around me at the men, I feel that God never meant us women to be too particular.
—Marie Jenney Howe, from *The Anti-Suffrage Monologue*

The Dramaturgs

MELISSA ATTEBERY began in Los Angeles in series television, holding various positions in production and development at companies like Paramount, Viacom and Granada Entertainment before moving to the New York stage, where she directs original people-driven plays for people with an edge. She produced *A Celebration of Women in Theatre: Miss Representation,* a rousing and thought-provoking evening of film, theatre, photography and discussion at The Players; and she is a co-producer and director with On Her Shoulders. She has evaluated scripts for the Atlantic Theater Company, New York Theatre Workshop and FringeNYC, and she holds both a BA in Dramatic Art and Film Studies from UC Santa Barbara and an MFA in Directing from the Actors Studio Drama School. She is an Associate Artistic Director and a resident director at Emerging Artists Theatre, a member of The Actors Studio Playwright/Director Workshop and the League of Professional Theatre Women and an Associate Member of the SDC. For updates on Melissa's upcoming projects, please visit: www.melissaattebery.com.

CELIA BRAXTON, Ph.D. is the Senior Dramaturg for NPTC's Women's Work Project, for which she co-leads a team of resident directors developing full-length scripts by 4-8 writers per season. Elsewhere, she has helped devise numerous one-person shows, including initial work with Stephanie Berry on her Obie-winning *The Shaneequa Chronicles,* and a dance/drama adaptation of *Macbeth* with the Avalon Theatre of e/Motion. Celia has presented at numerous academic conferences. Her NETJ article, "'Home, Sweet Home': The Drunkard, Domesticity, and the New Theatrical Audience," contextualizes the play within the climate of developing domestic ideology. She teaches in the Theatre program at LaGuardia Community College, and in the CUNY Start remedial education program at Queensborough Community College.

MELODY BROOKS has been producing and directing in NYC since 1983; in 1991 she founded New Perspectives Theatre Company and serves as Artistic Director and CEO. Its' mission and goals are a result of her long experience working in the Off- and Off-Off Broadway arenas. Melody directs the NPTC Women's Work LAB, which develops short and full-length plays by 12-15 members per year. She also serves as Executive Producer for NPTC'S *Voices From the Edge Festival,* which has showcased more than 75 new works by African-American writers since 1997 and of ON HER SHOULDERS, which presents the work of female playwrights through the ages in staged readings and scholarly playbills. Through these and other programs she has developed and directed numerous original and classic plays (with 2 OOBR Awards, an Audelco Award, a Princess Grace Finalist and Essence Entertainment Option among the honors the plays she has developed have received.) Melody received the "Spirit of Hope Award" in 2015 from Esperanza Theatre Company for her work with and support of women theatre artists for more than 25 years. She is a co-founder of 50/50 in 2020: Parity for Women Theatre Artists, and a member of the Board of Directors of the League of Professional Theatre Women. She also serves as co-chair of the LPTW Gilder-Coigney International Theatre Award for 2017.

BARBARA COHEN-STRATYNER, Ph. D., recently retired as Judy R. and Alfred A. Rosenberg Curator of Exhibitions at The New York Public Library for the Performing Arts. She has developed over 90 exhibitions on dance, theater, music, popular entertainments, photography, and design for The Library's galleries at Lincoln Center. Some have traveled across the country and to Berlin, China and Taiwan. She holds a BA from Barnard, an MFA in Theater Design and Ph. D. in Performance Studies from NYU, and an MS in the Leadership in Museum Education program at the Bank Street College of Education and has taught at CCNY and Parsons School of Design. She is the author of *Ned Wayburn and the Dance Routine, Touring West,* and author/editor of reference books on popular song, theater and dance. She remains active in exhibition development and the diversity and inclusion movement in the museum field.

MELISSA CONKLING most recently served as dramaturg on the development of *A Bad Night* by Nicole Pandolfo and Amy Witting. Previously, she was the dramaturg on *Sanctuary* at Theatre Row, the workshop production of *Road Veins* by Amy Witting, a staged reading of *The Convent of Pleasure* directed by Elyse Singer, and served as the dramaturgy apprentice on The Actors Company Theatre's 2014-2015 season. She participated in the 2015 Kennedy Center New Play Dramaturgy Incentive where she worked as an assistant dramaturg on *Vessels* by Matthew Capodicasa. In December 2015, she completed a Master of Arts in Theatre at Hunter College in Manhattan.

SHERRY ENGLE's publications ands conference papers reflect her ongoing interest in early women dramatists. Her book, *New Women Dramatists in America, 1880-1920* (New York: Palgrave Macmillan, 2007), focuses on American playwrights, Martha Morton, Madeleine Lucette Ryley, Beulah Marie Dix, Evelyn Greenleaf Sutherland and Rida Johnson Young. *Thousands of Noras; Short Plays by Women, 1 875-1920* (Bloomington,

IN: iUniverse, 2015) is an international collection coedited with British historian, Susan Croft. She also writes screenplays and plays, including a recent work *The 1936 Project*, a "living newspaper" production staged by theatre students and faculty at the Borough of Manhattan Community College. A member of the International Susan Glaspell Society and the Dramatists Guild, Sherry Engle is Associate Professor, in the Speech, Communications, and Theatre Arts Department at BMCC.

MARI LYN HENRY, author, teacher, image and career coach founded the Society for the Preservation of Theatrical History to reacquaint today's actors with the great actresses and visionaries of the 19th and early 20th centuries. www.SocietyPTH.com. Her workshops on on-camera techniques, script analysis, auditioning and impression management have been very successful in cities and universities across the country. Seminars about "The Business of the Business" are based on the best-selling book *How To Be A Working Actor*, she co-authored with Lynne Rogers. She teaches audition techniques and the business of acting at the Tom Todoroff Conservatory in New York and also at Circle in the Square. She is the director of the heritage program and a member of the League of Professional Theatre Women (www.theatrewomen.org). Her B.A. in Speech and Drama is from San Jose State University; M.A. in Theatre History from the Catholic University of America in Washington, D.C.

MORGAN JENNESS is a freelance dramaturg based in New York City For over 10 years, Jenness worked at the Public Theater, in roles ranging from literary manager to Director of Play Development to Associate Producer of the NY Shakespeare Festival. She was also Associate Artistic Director NYTW, and an Associate Director at the Los Angeles Theater Center in charge of new projects. She has worked with the Young Playwrights Festival, the Mark Taper Forum, The Playwrights Center/Playlabs, Bay Area Playwrights Festival, Double Image/New York Stage and Film, CSC, Victory Gardens, Hartford Stage, and Center Stage as a dramaturg, workshop director, and/or artistic consultant. She is currently on the faculty at Fordham University at Lincoln Center, where she teaches Theater History also having taught as a visiting artist or adjunct faculty at Bread Loaf, Brown University, Columbia University, University of Iowa, Pace University and New York University. In 1998 Jenness joined Helen Merrill Ltd. as Creative Director. She is now at Abrams Artist Agency as a consultant via This Distracted Globe Consultancy. In 2003, she received an Obie Award Special Citation for Longtime Support of Playwrights. In 2015 the Literary Managers and Dramaturgs of the Americas presented the G. E. Lessing Award to Jenness for lifetime achievement in the field of dramaturgy.

SUSAN JONAS is a dramaturg, playwright, producer, director and administrator. She held leadership positions at The Acting Company, Classical Stage Company and Classical Theatre of Harlem, and taught at New York University, Ithaca College, University of New Hampshire and Princeton. Her adaptations have been produced in New York and regionally, her articles published in *American Theatre*, and for twenty years *Dramaturgy and American Theatre*, which she co-edited, was the primary textbook in the field. While Theatre Arts Analyst at New York State Council on the Arts, she co-wrote the groundbreaking "Report on the Status of Women in Theatre." Partnering with N.Y.U., C.U.N.Y., Princeton and The New School, she worked to restore women's contribution to the living repertory, founding *The Legacy Project*, and co-founding both *50/50 in 2020* (awarded the 2010 *New York Theatre Experience Person of the Year)* and "On Her Shoulders," curating its inaugural season. Her D.F.A. was awarded by Yale School of Drama.

SHANA KOMITEE joined the Julliard Drama Division in 2012, the inaugural year of the MFA program, and is also on faculty in the Evening Division. She teaches theater history and literature and provides dramaturgy for all Drama Division performances. Before coming to Juilliard, Ms. Komitee lived in and wrote about ethnic conflict in Northern Ireland and worked at the Center for Jewish-Arab Economic Development in Tel Aviv. After four years in the Middle East, Ms. Komitee returned to the United States to pursue a joint MA/PhD at Harvard University in Near Eastern Languages and Civilizations and Performance Studies. She was awarded four Harvard University Bok Center Certificates of Distinction in undergraduate teaching fellowship. Ms. Komitee is the author of *A Student's Guide to Performance Studies* and the text for the first Juilliard Open Studios episode on Tony Kushner's *Angels in America,* among other works. Outside Juilliard, Ms. Komitee provides dramaturgy at various New York City theaters, including most recently Manhattan Theatre Club and the Pearl Theatre Company.

ANDREA LEPCIO is best known for *Looking for the Pony* a finalist for the Dramatists Guild Hull-Warriner Award and NEA Outstanding New American Play Award. Upcoming productions include *Strait of Gibraltar* at Sinchronicity Theatre in Georgia and American Stage in Florida and *Tunnel Vision* at Venus Theatre in Maryland. Andrea is a Dramatists Guild fellow and served as the Fellows program director for 10 years. M.F.A., Carnegie Mellon University. B.A. Human Ecology, College of the Atlantic.

LOREN NOVECK is a writer and dramaturg, and was the literary manager of Six Figures Theatre Company, where she also co-produced the Artists of Tomorrow Festival and other show. She is the cowriter of *Girl Blog from Iraq: Baghdad Burning,* and has written theater reviews and features for nytheatre.com, *The Brooklyn Rail, Exeunt* magazine, and *The Brooklyn Paper.*

SADAH ESPII PROCTOR is a dramaturg, performer, and sound & media designer based in Brooklyn, New York. She collaborates with artists and technologists in developing immersive, interactive, and performative experiences. Her work is influenced by visual kei, cyberpunk, and Afrofuturist movements, exploring themes of womanism, social justice, rhythm and movement, and cultural aspects of the African Diaspora. Through the use of gestural sound, spatialized audio, and physical computing, she aims to create a "cyborg theatre" that integrates the body with technology in live performance. B.A. Theatre Arts, Virginia Tech. M.F.A. candidate ('17) Performance & Interactive Media Arts, Brooklyn College. Website: sadahespiiproctor.com.

TASHA GORDON SOLOMON's plays have been developed and produced at Actors Theater of Louisville, Clubbed Thumb, Dixon Place, Perry Mansfield New Works Festival, The Humana Festival, New Georges, Ars Nova and The Flea. She is a recipient of the Dramatist Guild Fellowship, a lyricist in the BMI Workshop, a New Georges Affiliated Artist, a member of the Project Y Playwrights Group and an alumna of the Ars Nova Playgroup and Clubbed Thumb's Emerging Writers Group. Her writing has been published in *The Brooklyn Rail, The Dramatist,* and *The Huffington Post.* Tasha has directed new plays at Ensemble Studio Theatre, The Tank, The Brick, The Cell, The Signature Ford Studio, Pipeline Theatre, Studio Tisch, Columbia University, the New York Fringe Festival, the Fire This Time Festival, and the Young Playwrights Festival. Tasha received her MFA in Dramatic Writing at NYU, attended the National Theater Institute, and is a proud 52nd Street Project volunteer.

ARMINDA THOMAS served as dramaturg and archivist for Dee-Davis Enterprises, where her production dramaturgy credits include Ossie Davis' *A Last Dance for Sybil* (New Federal Theater) and Ruby Dee's musical adaptation of *John Boscoe and the Devil* (EST's Going to the River festival). Additional dramaturgy credits include *The First Noel* (Classical Theatre of Harlem), *Shakespeare's Women* (Hattiloo, Memphis), *Bitter Fruit* (San Francisco), and the Obie-award winning production of *June and Jean in Concert* (Signature Theatre). She also served as archival consultant for the documentary *Life's Essentials With Ruby Dee* and executive producer for the Grammy-award winning audio book With Ossie and Ruby: *In This Life Together* (Hachette). She is resident dramaturg for the Going to the River Writer's Unit, and holds an MFA in dramaturgy and script development from Columbia University.

HEATHER VIOLANTI is a New York-based dramaturg and playwright. Favorite credits include dramaturgy for four wonderful plays written by women and produced by the Mint Theater: *A Little Journey* and *Susan and God* by Rachel Crothers, *So Help Me God!* by Maurine Dallas Watkins, and *Love Goes to Press* by Martha Gellhorn and Virginia Cowles . She also contributed articles to the education guide for the Broadway musical *Allegiance* and research to the BBC's genealogically-themed program *Who Do You Think You Are?*. She has worked with emerging playwrights in developing their plays in England and the United States. She is currently a member of the BMI Librettists Workshop. Heather holds an MFA in Dramaturgy and Dramatic Criticism from the Yale School of Drama and an MA, Writing for Stage and Broadcast Media, from the Royal Central School of Speech and Drama.

ELIZABETH WHITNEY is an Assistant Professor in the City University of New York at Borough of Manhattan Community College in the Department of Speech, Communication & Theatre Arts. During the 2015-2016 academic year she was a Fulbright Scholar at University of Turku in Finland, in the Department of Media Studies, researching arts funding and freedom of expression. A Performance Studies scholar/practitioner, her research appears in *Text and Performance Quarterly* and *Liminalities: A Journal of Performance Studies*. Her lecture performance, *Queer Longing, Queer Failure: A Performative Lecture on Anna Elizabeth Dickinson*, was developed with support from the National Endowment for the Humanities, the Gilder Lehrman Foundation, and the Faculty Resource Network Scholar in Residence Program at New York University. She is a member of the alt-country camp feminist trio, Menage a Twang. For more info www.elizabethjwhitney.com.

The On Her Shoulders Team

New Perspectives Theatre Company (NPTC) is an award-winning company founded in 1991 as a multi-racial ensemble dedicated to using theatre as an agent for positive social change. Our mission is to 1) develop and present new plays and playwrights, particularly women and people of color, 2) present classic plays in a style that sheds new light on our lives and work, and 3) offer theatre and its benefits to under-served audiences—especially young people and communities in need—to build life skills and promote positive participation in our society. **Our aim is not to exclude, but to cast a wider net.** In all of our work, we seek to share our vision of a united future, in which differences, particularly ethnic or cultural, are seen as added flavor to the melting pot and not as unwanted or unnecessary ingredients. NPTC co-founded **50/50 in 2020: Parity for Women Theatre Artists** in 2009, a grassroots movement of women theatre professionals and their advocates, with the mission of achieving employment parity by the centennial of winning suffrage. This led to an increased interest in reclaiming the full heritage of women theatre artists throughout history, via research and performance events, and an expanded array of projects, including ON HER SHOULDERS.

THE SCHOOL OF DRAMA AT THE NEW SCHOOL: The creative home for the future of performing arts. Agile. Engaged. Innovative. Multidisciplinary. The School of Drama at The New School is home to a dynamic group of young directors, writers, actors, and creative technologists and an award-winning faculty. Our playwriting, directing, and acting school in New York City brings together rigor, creativity, and collaborative learning across performance disciplines to create work marked by professionalism, imagination, and civic awareness. For more information, please visit www.newschool.edu/drama.

The Play in Context, the dramaturgical and scholarly presentation component to the program, is sponsored in part by the **League of Professional Theatre Women** (LPTW), a non-profit advocacy organization with a mission to reinforce the positive image of, promote the visibility of, and increase opportunities for women in the professional theatre. Incorporated in 1986, LPTW today is a major support system for theatre women in all disciplines, as well as the professions that keep the business of theatre operating. In addition to the foundational activities of networking and collaboration, programs include panel discussions, career workshops, educational symposia, historical exhibitions, field-wide publications, and awards recognizing distinguished women leaders. The current membership numbers nearly 500 women in the commercial and nonprofit sectors from around the city, the country and the world.

CPSIA information can be obtained
at www.ICGtesting.com
Printed in the USA
BVOW07s0940120417
480980BV00009B/6/P